Jewel Mysteries I Have Known: From A Dealer's Note Book

Max Pemberton

JEWEL MYSTERIES

I HAVE KNOWN

From a Dealer's Note Book

BY

MAX PEMBERTON

Author of "The Iron Pirate," etc

ILLUSTRATED BY

R. CATON WOODVILLE AND FRED BARNARD

LONDON

WARD, LOCK & CO LIMITED

WARWICK HOUSE SALISBURY SQUARE EC

NEW YORK AND MELBOURNE

JEWEL MYSTERIES I HAVE KNOWN

"'AH, MACLAREN, SO THAT'S YOU—DEVILISH GOOD OF YOU TO COME
ABOARD, I MUST SAY.'"

[See page 126.

CONTENTS

THE OPAL OF CARMALOVITCH

THE OPAL OF CARMALOVITCH

DARK was falling from a dull and humid sky, and the lamps were beginning to struggle for brightness in Piccadilly, when the opal of Carmalovitch was first put into my hand. The day had been a sorry one for business: no light, no sun, no stay of the downpour of penetrating mist which had been swept through the city by the driving south wind from the late dawn to the mock of sunset. I had sat in my private office for six long hours, and had not seen a customer. The umbrella-bearing throng which trod the street before my window hurried quickly through the mud and the slush, as people who had no leisure even to gaze upon precious stones they could not buy. I was going home, in fact, as the one sensible proceeding on such an afternoon, and had my hand upon the great safe to shut it, when the mirror above my desk showed me the reflection of a curious-looking man who had entered the outer shop, and stood already at the counter.

At the first glance I judged that this man was no ordinary customer. His dress was altogether singular. He had a black coat covering him from his neck to his heels—a coat half-smothered in astrachan, and one

which could have been made by no English tailor. But
his hands were ungloved, and he wore a low hat, which
might have been the hat of an office boy. I could see
from the little window of my private room, which gives
my eye command of the shop, that he had come on foot,
and for lack of any umbrella was pitiably wet. Yet
there was fine bearing about him, and he was clearly
a man given to command, for my assistant mounted to
my room with his name at the first bidding.

"Does he say what he wants?" I asked, reading the
large card upon which were the words—

"STENILOFF CARMALOVITCH";

but the man replied,—

"Only that he must see you immediately. I don't like
the look of him at all."

"Is Abel in the shop?"

"He's at the door."

"Very well; let him come to the foot of my stairs,
and if I ring as usual, both of you come up."

In this profession of jewel-selling—for every calling
is a profession nowadays—we are so constantly cheek
by jowl with swindlers that the coming of one more or
less is of little moment in a day's work. At my own
place of business the material and personal precautions
are so organised that the cleverest scoundrel living
would be troubled to get free of the shop with sixpenny-
worth of booty on him. I have two armed men ready at
the ring of my bell—Abel is one of them—and a private
wire to the nearest police-station. From an alcove well
hidden on the right hand of the lower room, a man
watches by day the large cases where the smaller gems
are shown, and by night a couple of special guards
have charge of the safe and the premises. I touch a

bell twice in my room, and my own detective follows
any visitor who gives birth in my mind to the slightest
doubt. I ring three times, and any obvious impostor is
held prisoner until the police come. These things are
done by most jewellers in the West End; there is nothing in them either unusual or fearful. There are so
many professed swindlers—so many would-be snappers
up of unconsidered and considerable trifles—that precautions such as I have named are the least that common
sense and common prudence will allow one to take. And
they have saved me from loss, as they have saved
others again and again.

I had scarce given my instructions to Michel, my
assistant—a rare reader of intention, and a fine judge of
faces—when the shabby-genteel man entered. Michel
placed a chair for him on the opposite side of my desk,
and then left the room. There was no more greeting
between the new-comer and myself than a mutual nod-
ding of heads; and he on his part fell at once upon his
business. He took a large paper parcel from the inside
pocket of his coat and began to unpack it; but there was
so much paper, both brown and tissue, that I had some
moments of leisure in which to examine him more
closely before we got to talk. I set him down in my
mind as a man hovering on the boundary line of the
middle age, a man with infinite distinction marked in a
somewhat worn face, and with some of the oldest clothes
under the shielding long coat that I have ever looked
upon. These I saw when he unbuttoned the enveloping
cape to get at his parcel in the inner pocket; and while
he undid it, I could observe that his fingers were thin as
the talons of a bird, and that he trembled all over with
the mere effort of unloosing the string.

The operation lasted some minutes. He spoke no

word during that time, but when he had reduced the
coil of brown paper to a tiny square of wash-leather, I
asked him,—

"Have you something to show me?"

He looked up at me with a pair of intensely, ridiculously blue eyes, and shrugged his shoulders.

"Should I undo all these-papers if I had not?" he
responded; and I saw at once that he was a man who,
from a verbal point of view, stood objectionably upon
the defensive.

"What sort of a stone is it?" I went on in a somewhat
uninterested tone of voice; "not a ruby, I hope. I have
just bought a parcel of rubies."

By way of answer he opened the little wash-leather
bag, and taking up my jewel-tongs, which lay at his hand,
he held up an opal of such prodigious size and quality
that I restrained myself with difficulty from crying out
at the sight of it. It was a Cerwenitza stone, I saw at
a glance, almost a perfect circle in shape, and at least
four inches in diameter. There was a touch of the oxide
in its colour which gave it the faintest suspicion of
black in the shade of its lights; but for wealth of hue
and dazzling richness in its general quality, it surpassed
any stone I have known, even that in the imperial cabinet at Vienna. So brilliant was it, so fascinating in
the ever-changing play of its amazing variegations, so
perfect in every characteristic of the finest Hungarian
gems, that for some moments I let the man hold it out to
me, and said no word. There was running through my
mind the question which must have arisen under such circumstances: Where had he got it from? He had stolen it,
I concluded at the first thought; and again, at the second,
How else could a man who wore rags under an astrachan coat have come to the possession of a gem upon

which the most commercial instinct would have hesitated to set a price?

I had fully determined that I was face to face with a swindler, when his exclamation reminded me that he expected me to speak.

" ' WELL,' HE SAID, ' ARE YOU FRIGHTENED TO LOOK AT IT ? ' "

"Well," he said, "are you frightened to look at it?"

He had been holding out the tongs, in which he gripped the stone lightly, for some seconds, and I had not yet ventured to touch them, sitting, I do not doubt, with surprise written all over my face. But when he spoke,

I took the opal from him, and turned my strong glass upon it.

"You seem to have brought me a fine thing," I said as carelessly as I could. "Is it a stone with a history?"

"It has no history—at least, none that I should care to write."

"And yet," I continued, "there cannot be three larger opals in Europe; do you know the stone at Vienna?"

"Perfectly; but it has not the black of this, and is coarser. This is an older stone, so far as the birth of its discovery goes, by a hundred years."

I thought that he was glib with his tale for a man who had such a poor one; and certainly he looked me in the face with amazing readiness. He had not the eyes of a rogue, and his manner was not that of one criminally restless.

"If you will allow me," I said, when I had looked at the stone for a few moments, "I will examine this under the brighter light there; perhaps you would like to amuse yourself with this parcel of rubies."

This was a favourite little trick of mine. I had two or three parcels of stones to show to any man who came to me labouring under a sorry and palpably poor story; and one of these I then took from my desk and spread upon the table under the eyes of the Russian. The stones were all imitation, and worth no more than six-pence apiece. If he were a judge, he would discover the cheat at the first sight of them; if he were a swindler, he would endeavour to steal them. In either case the test was useful. And I took care to turn my back upon him while I examined the opal, to give him every opportunity of filling his pockets should he choose.

When I had the jewel under the powerful light of an unshaded incandescent lamp I could see that it merited all the appreciation I had bestowed upon it at first sight. It was flawless, wanting the demerit of a single mark which could be pointed to in depreciation of its price. For play of colour and radiating generosity of hues, I have already said that no man has seen its equal. I put it in the scales, called Michel to establish my own opinions, tried it by every test that can be applied to a gem so fragile and so readily harmed, and came to the only conclusion possible—that it was a stone which would make a sensation in any market, and call bids from all the courts in Europe. It remained for me to learn the history of it, and with that I went back to my desk and resumed the conversation, first glancing at the sham parcel of rubies, to find that the man had not even looked at them.

"It is a remarkable opal," I said; "the finest ever put before me. You have come here to sell it, I presume?"

"Exactly. I want five thousand pounds for it."

"And if I make you a bid you are prepared to furnish me with the history both of it and of yourself?"

He shrugged his shoulders contemptuously. "If you think that I have stolen it we had better close the discussion at once. I am not prepared to tell my history to every tradesman I deal with."

"In that case," said I, "you have wasted your time. I buy no jewels that I do not know all about."

His superciliousness was almost impertinent. It would have been quite so if it had not been dominated by an absurd and almost grotesque pride, which accounted for his temper. I was sure then that he was either an honest man or the best actor I had ever seen.

"Think the matter over," I added in a less indifferent tone; "I am certain that you will then acquit me of unreasonableness. Call here again in a day or two, and we will have a chat about it."

This softer speech availed me as little as the other. He made no sort of answer to it, but packing his opal carefully again, he rose abruptly and left the shop. As he went I touched my bell twice, and Abel followed him quietly down Piccadilly, while I sent a line to Scotland Yard informing the Commissioners of the presence of such a man as the Russian in London, and of the Gargantuan jewel which he carried. Then I went home through the fog and the humid night; but my way was lighted by a memory of the magnificent gem I had seen, and the hunger for the opal was already upon me.

The inquiry at Scotland Yard proved quite futile. The police telegraphed to Paris, to Berlin, to St. Petersburg, to New York, but got no tidings either of a robbery or of the man whom mere circumstances pointed at as a pretender. This seemed to me the more amazing since I could not conceive that a stone such as this was should not have made a sensation in some place. Jewels above all material things do not hide their light under bushels. Let there be a great find at Kimberley or in the Burmese mines; let a fine emerald or a perfect turquoise be brought to Europe, and every dealer in the country knows its weight, its colour, and its value before three days have passed. If this man, who hugged this small fortune to him, and without it was a beggar, had been a worker at Cerwenitza, he would have told me the fact plainly. But he spoke of the opal being older even than the famous and commonly cited specimen at Vienna. How came it that he alone had the history of such an ancient gem? There was only one answer to such a question—the history of his possession of it, at any rate, would not bear inquiry.

Such perplexity was not removed by Abel's account of his journey after Carmalovitch. He had followed the man from Piccadilly to Oxford Circus; thence, after a long wait in Regent's Park, where the Russian sat for at least an hour on a seat near the Botanical Gardens

ABEL AT WORK.

entrance, to a small house in Boscobel Place. This was evidently a lodging-house, offering that fare of shabbiness and dirt which must perforce be attractive to the needy. There was a light burning at the window of the pretentiously poor drawing-room when the man arrived, and a girl, apparently not more than twenty-five years of age, came down into the hall to greet him, the pair afterwards showing at the window for a moment before the blinds were drawn. An inquiry by my man for apartments in the house elicited only a shrill cackle and a negative from a shuffling hag who answered the knock. A tour of the little shops in the neighbourhood provided the further clue "that they paid for nothing." This suburban estimation of personal worth was a confirmation of my conclusion drawn from the rags beneath the astrachan coat. The Russian was a poor man; except for the possession of the jewel he was near to being a beggar. And yet he had not sought to borrow money of me, and he had put the price of £5,000 upon his property.

All these things did not leave my mind for the next week. I was in daily communication with Scotland Yard, but absolutely to no purpose. Their sharpest men handled the case, and confessed that they could make nothing of it. We had the house in Boscobel Place watched, but, so far as we could learn, Carmalovitch, as he called himself, never left it. Meanwhile, I began to think that I had betrayed exceedingly poor judgment in raising the question at all. As the days went by I suffered that stone hunger which a student of opals alone can know. I began to believe that I had lost by my folly one of the greatest possessions that could come to a man in my business. I knew that it would be an act of childishness to go to the house and re-open the negotiations, for I could not bid for that which the first telegram from the Continent might prove to be feloniously gotten, and the embarkation of such a sum as was asked was a matter not for the spur of the moment, but for the closest deliberation, to say nothing of financial preparation. Yet I would have given fifty pounds if the owner of it

had walked into my office again ; and I never heard a
footstep in the outer shop during the week following his
visit but I looked up in the hope of seeing him.

A fortnight passed, and I thought that I had got to the
beginning and the end of the opal mystery, when one
morning, the moment after I had entered my office, Michel
told me that a lady wished to see me. I had scarce time
to tell him that I could see no one for an hour when the
visitor pushed past him into the den, and sat herself
down in the chair before my writing-desk. As in all
business, we appreciate, and listen to, impertinence in
the jewel trade ; and when I observed the magnificent
impudence of the young lady, I asked Michel to leave us,
and waited for her to speak. She was a delicate-
looking woman—an Italian, I thought, from the dark
hue of her skin and the lustrous beauty of her eyes—
but she was exceedingly shabbily dressed, and her hands
were ungloved. She was not a woman you would have
marked in the stalls of a theatre as the fit subject for an
advertising photographer ; but there was great sweetness in her face, and those signs of bodily weakness and
want of strength which so often enhance a woman's
beauty. When she spoke, although she had little English, her voice was well modulated and remarkably
pleasing.

"You are Monsieur Bernard Sutton?" she asked,
putting one hand upon my table, and the other between
the buttons of her bodice.

I bowed in answer to her.

"You have met my husband—I am Madame Carmalovitch—he was here, it is fifteen days, to sell you an opal.
I have brought it again to you now, for I am sure you
wish to buy it."

"You will pardon me," I said, "but I am waiting for

the history of the jewel which your husband promised me. I rather expected that he would have sent it."

" 'YOU ARE MONSIEUR BERNARD SUTTON?' SHE ASKED."

"I know! oh, I know so well; and I have asked him many times," she answered; "but you can believe me, he will tell of his past to no one, not even to me. But he is honest and true; there is not such a man in all your city—and he has suffered. You may buy this beautiful thing now, and you will never regret it. I tell you so from all my heart."

"But surely, Madame," said I, "you must see that I cannot pay such a price as your husband is asking for his property if he will not even tell me who he is, or where he comes from."

" Yes, that is it—not even to me has he spoken of these things. I was married to him six years now at Naples, and he has always had the opal which he offers to you. We were rich then, but we have known suffering, and this alone is left to us. You will buy it of my husband, for you in all this London are the man to buy it. It will give you fame and money.; it must give you both, for we ask but four thousand pounds for it.".

I started at this. Here was a drop of a thousand pounds upon the price asked but fifteen days ago. What did it mean? I took up the gem, which the woman had placed upon the table, and saw in a moment. The stone was dimming. It had lost colour since I had seen it; it had lost, too, I judged, at least one-third of its value. I had heard the old woman's tales of the capricious change-fulness of this remarkable gem, but it was the first time that I had ever witnessed for myself such an unmistake-able depreciation. The woman read the surprise in my eyes, and answered my thoughts, herself thoughtful, and her dark eyes touched with tears.

" You see what I see," she said. " The jewel that you have in your hand is the index to my husband's life. He has told me so often. When he is well, it is well; when hope has come to him, the lights which shine there are as the light of his hope. When he is ill, the opal fades;

when he dies, it will die too. That is what I believe and he believes; it is what his father told him when he gave him the treasure, nearly all that was left of a great fortune."

This tale astounded me; it betrayed absurd superstition, but it was the first ray of coherent explanation which had been thrown upon the case. I took up the thread with avidity and pursued it.

"Your husband's father was a rich man?" I asked. "Is he dead?"

She looked up with a start, then dropped her eyes quickly, and mumbled something. Her hesitation was so marked that I put her whole story from me as a clever fabrication, and returned again to the theory of robbery.

"Madame," I said, "unless your husband can add to that which you tell me, I shall be unable to purchase your jewel."

"Oh, for the love of God don't say that!" she cried; "we are so poor, we have hardly eaten for days! Come and see Monsieur Carmalovitch and he shall tell you all; I implore you, and you will never regret this kindness! My husband is a good friend; he will reward your friendship. You will not refuse me this?"

It is hard to deny a pretty woman; it is harder still when she pleads with tears in her voice. I told her that I would go and see her husband on the following evening at nine o'clock, and counselled her to persuade him in the between time to be frank with me, since frankness alone could avail him. She accepted my advice with gratitude, and left as she had come, her pretty face made handsomer by its look of gloom and pensiveness. Then I fell to thinking upon the wisdom, or want of wisdom, in the promise I had given. Stories of men drugged, or robbed, or murdered by jewel thieves crowded upon my mind, but always with the recollection that I should carry nothing to Boscobel Place. A man who had no more upon him than a well-worn suit of clothes and a Swiss lever watch in a silver case, such as I carry invariably, would scarce be quarry for the most venturesome shop-hawk that the history of knavery has made known to us. I could risk nothing by going to the house, I was sure; but I might get the opal, and for that I longed still with a fever for possession which could only be accounted for by the beauty of the gem.

Being come to this determination, I left my own house in a hansom-cab on the following evening at half-past eight o'clock, taking Abel with me, more after my usual custom than from any prophetic alarm. I had money upon me sufficient only for the payment of the cab; and I took the extreme precaution of putting aside the diamond ring that I had been wearing during the day. As I live in Bayswater, it was but a short drive across Paddington Green and down the Marylebone Road to Boscobel Place; and when we reached the house we found it lighted up on the drawing-room floor as Abel had seen it at his first going there. But the hall was quite in darkness, and I had to ring twice before the shrill-voiced dame I had heard of answered to my knock. She carried a frousy candle in her hand; and was so uncanny-looking that I motioned to Abel to keep a watch from the outside upon the house before I went upstairs to that which was a typical lodging-house room. There was a " tapestry " sofa against one wall ; half a dozen chairs in evident decline stood in hilarious attitudes ; some seaweed, protected for no obvious reason by shades of glass, decorated the mantelpiece, and a sampler displayed the obviously aggravating advice to a tenant of such a place, " Waste not, want not." But the rickety writing-table was strewn with papers, and there was half a cigar lying upon the edge of it, and a cup of coffee there had grown cold in the dish.

The aspect of the place amazed me. I began to regret that I had set out upon any such enterprise, but had no time to draw back before the Russian entered. He wore an out-at-elbow velvet coat, and the rest of his dress was shabby enough to suit his surroundings. I noticed, however, that he offered me a seat with a gesture that was superb, and that his manner was less agitated than it had been at our first meeting.

" I am glad to see you," he said.   " You have come to buy my opal ? "

" Under certain conditions, yes."

" That is very good of you; but I am offering you a great bargain.   My price for the stone now is £3,000, one thousand less than my wife offered it at yesterday."

" It has lost more of its colour, then ? "

" Decidedly ; or I should not have lowered my claim— but see for yourself."

He took the stone from the wash-leather bag, and laid it upon the writing-table. I started with amazement and sorrow at the sight of it. The glorious lights I had admired not twenty days ago were half gone ; a dull, salty-red tinge was creeping over the superb green and the scintillating black which had made me covet the jewel with such longing. Yet it remained, even in its comparative poverty, the most remarkable gem I have ever put hand upon.

" The stone is certainly going off," I said in answer to him.   " What guarantee have I that it will not be worthless in a month's time ? "

" You have my word.   It is a tradition of our family

that he who owns that heirloom when it begins to fade must sell it or die—and sell it at its worth. If I continue to possess it, the tradition must prove itself, for I shall die of sheer starvation."

"And if another has it?"

"It will regain its lights, I have no doubt of it, for it has gone like this before when a death has happened amongst us. If you are content to take my word, I will return to you in six months' time and make good any loss you have suffered by it. But I should want some money now, to-night, before an hour—could you let me have it?"

"If I bought your stone, you could have the money for it; my man, who is outside, would fetch my cheque-book."

At the word "man," he went to the window, and saw Abel standing beneath the gas-lamp. He looked fixedly at the fellow for a moment, and then drew down the blinds in a deliberate way which I did not like at all.

"That servant of yours has been set to watch this house for ten days," he said. "Was that by your order?"

I was so completely taken aback by his discovery that I sat for a moment dumbfounded, and gave him no answer. He, however, seemed trembling with passion.

"Was it by your orders?" he asked again, standing over me and almost hissing out his words.

"It was," I answered after a pause; "but, you see, circumstances were suspicious."

"Suspicious! Then you *did* believe me to be a rogue. I have shot men for less."

I attempted to explain, but he would not hear me. He

had lost command of himself, stalking up and down the room with great strides until the temper tautened his veins, and his lean hands seemed nothing but wire and bones. At last, he took a revolver from the drawer in his table, and deliberately put cartridges into it. I stood up at the sight of it and made a step towards the window ; but he pointed the pistol straight at me, crying,—

" Sit down, if you wish to live another minute—and say, do you still believe me to be a swindler ?"

The situation was so dangerous, for the man was obviously but half sane, that I do not know what I said in answer to him ; yet he pursued my words fiercely, scarce hearing my reply before he continued,—

" You have had my house watched, and, as I know now, you have branded my name before the police as that of a criminal ; you shall make atonement here on the spot by buying that opal, or you do not leave the room alive ! "

It was a desperate trial, and I sat for some minutes as a man on the borderland of death. Had I been sensible then and fenced with him in his words, I should now possess the opal ; but I let out the whole of my thoughts—and the jewel went with them.

" I cannot buy your stone," I said, " until I have your history and your father's——" But I said no more, for at the mention of his father he cried out like a wounded beast, and fired the revolver straight at my head. The shot skinned my forehead and the powder behind it blackened my face ; but I had no other injury, and I sprang upon him.

For some moments the struggle was appalling. I had him gripped about the waist with my left arm, my right

"'SIT DOWN, IF YOU WISH TO LIVE ANOTHER MINUTE.'"

clutching the hand wherein he held the pistol. He, in turn, put his left hand upon my throat and threw his right leg round mine with a sinewy strength that amazed me. Thus we were, rocking like two trees blown in a gale, now swaying towards the window, now to the door, now crashing against the table, or hurling the papers and the ink and the ornaments in a confused heap, as, fighting the ground foot by foot, we battled for the mastery. But I could not cry out, for his grip about my neck was the grip of a maniac; and as it tightened and tightened, the light grew dim before my eyes and I felt that I was choking. This he knew, and with overpowering fury pressed his fingers upon my throat until he cut me with his nails as with knives. Then, at last, I reeled from the agony of it; and we fell with tremendous force under the window, he uppermost.

Of that lifelong minute that followed, I remember but little. I know only that he knelt upon my chest, still gripping my throat with his left hand, and began to reach out for his revolver, which had dropped beneath the table in our struggle. I had just seen him reach it with his finger-tips, and so draw it inch by inch towards him, when a fearful scream rang out in the room, and his hand was stayed. The scream was from the woman who had come to Piccadilly the day before, and it was followed by a terrible paroxysm of weeping, and then by a heavy fall, as the terrified girl fainted. He let me go at this, and stood straight up; but at the first step towards his wife he put his foot upon the great opal, which we had thrown to the ground in our encounter, and he crushed it into a thousand fragments.

When he saw what he had done, one cry, and one alone, escaped from him; but before I could raise a hand

"HE HAD TURNED THE PISTOL TO HIS HEAD AND BLOWN HIS BRAINS OUT,"

to stay him, he had turned the pistol to his head, and had blown his brains out.

*   *   *   *   *

The story of the opal of Carmalovitch is almost told. A long inquiry after the man's death added these facts to the few I had already gleaned. He was the son of a banker in Buda-Pesth, a noble Russian, who had emigrated to Hungary and taken his wealth with him to embark it in his business. He himself had been educated partly in England, partly in France; but at the moment when he should have entered the great firm in Buda-Pesth, there came the Argentine crash, and his father was one of those who succumbed. But he did more than succumb, he helped himself to the money of his partners, and being discovered, was sentenced as a common felon, and is at this moment in a Hungarian prison.

Steniloff, the son, was left to clear up the estate, and got from it, when all was settled, a few thousand pounds, by the generosity of the father's partners. Beyond these he had the opal, which the family had possessed for three hundred years, buying it originally in Vienna. This possession, however, had, for the sake of some absurd tradition, always been kept a profound secret, and when the great crash came, the man whose death I had witnessed took it as his fortune. For some years he had lived freely, at Rome, at Nice, at Naples, where he married; but his money being almost spent, he brought his wife to England, and there attempted to sell the jewel. As he would tell nothing of his history, lest his father's name should suffer, he found no buyer, and dragged on from month to month, going deeper in the byways of poverty until he came to me. The rest I have told you.

Of the opal which I saw so woefully crushed in the lodging-house in Boscobel Place, but one large fragment remained. I have had that set in a ring, and have sold it to-day for fifty pounds. The money will go to Madame Carmalovitch, who has returned to her parents in Naples. She has suffered much.

THE NECKLACE OF GREEN DIAMONDS

THE NECKLACE OF GREEN DIAMONDS

I CAN remember perfectly well the day upon which I received the order from my eccentric old friend, Francis Brewer, to make him a necklace of green diamonds. It was the 2nd of May in the year 1890, exactly three days after his marriage with the fascinating little singer, Eugenie Clarville, who had set Paris aflame with the piquancy of her acting and her delightful command of a fifth-rate voice some six months after Brewer had left London to take up the management of a great banking enterprise in the French capital. He was then well into the forties; but he had skipped through life with scarce a jostle against the venial sins, and was as ignorant as a babe where that mortal septette of vices which the clergy anathematise on the first Wednesday in Lent was concerned,

I have never known a more childish man, or one who held your affection so readily with simplicity. He was large-hearted, trusting, boyish, by no means unintellectual, and in no sense a fool. Indeed, his commercial knowledge was highly valuable; and his energy in working up a business was a reproach to those who, like myself, love to sit in arm-chairs and watch the ebb of life from a plate-glass window.

When he was married he wrote to me, and I laid his letter upon my table with a whistle. Not that he was in any way suited for the celibate state, for his instinct was wholly cast in the marrying mould. Had I been called upon to paint him, I should have sat him in an arm-chair by the side of a roaring fire, with a glass of punch to toast a buxom goodwife, and a pipe as long as the stick of my umbrella to make rings of smoke for a new generation at his knee. Such a man should, said common sense, have been yoked to an English dame, to one used to the odour of the lemon, and motherly by instinct and by training. I could not imagine him married to a lady from the Vaudeville; the contrast between his iron-headed directness and the gauze and tinsel of opera bouffe seemed grotesque almost to incredulity. Yet there was the letter, and there were his absurd ravings about a woman he had known distantly for six months, and intimately for three days.

"I have married," he said in this memorable communication, "the dearest little soul that God ever brought into the world—fresh as the breeze, bright as the sky, eyes like the night, and temper like an angel. You must come and see her, old boy, the moment we set foot in our house at Villemomble. I shan't let you lose an hour; you must learn for yourself what a magnificent Benedick I make. Why, the days go like flashes of the

"THE GREAT TRAIN SMASH NEAR ROUEN."

sun—and there never was a happier man in or out of
this jolly city. Oh, you slow-goers in London, you poor
lame cab-horses, what do you know of life or of woman,
or even of the sky above you? Come to Paris, old man ;
come, I say, and we'll put you through your paces, and
you shall meet her, the very best little wife that ever
fell to an old dray-horse in this fair of high-steppers."

There was a good deal more of this sort of thing ; but
the kernel of the letter was in a postscriptum, as was
the essence of most of his communications. He told me
there that he desired to make some substantial present
to the girl he had just married ; and he inclosed a rough
sketch of a necklace which he thought would be a pretty
thing if rare stones were used to decorate it. I fell in
with his whim at once ; and as it chanced that I had just
received from the Jägersfontein mine a parcel of twenty
very fine greenish diamonds, I determined to use them
in the business. I may say that these stones were of a
delicious pale green tint, almost the colour of the great
jewel in the vaults at Dresden, and that their fire was
amazing. I have known a gem of the hue to be worth
nearly a hundred pounds a carat ; and as the lot I had
averaged two carats apiece, their worth was very considerable. I had not learnt what were Brewer's instructions in the matter of expense ; but I wrote to him by
the next post congratulating him on his marriage and
informing him that I would set the green diamonds in a
necklace, and sell them for two thousand pounds. He
accepted the offer by a cablegram, and on the following
day sent a long letter of instruction, the pith of which
was the order to engrave on the inner side of the
pendant the words, *major lex amor est nobis.* I laughed
at his Latin, and the amatory exuberance which it
betrayed ; but fell upon the work, and finished it in the

course of three weeks, during which time I had many and irritating requests from him for constant and detailed accounts of its progress.

When the trinket reached him, his satisfaction was quite childish. He wrote of his delight, and of "Eugy's," and spoilt three sheets of good note-paper telling me of her appearance at the English ball early in June; and of the sensation such an extraordinary bauble caused. Then I heard from him no more until August, when I read in an evening paper that he had been returning from Veulettes after a short holiday, and had been in the great train smash near Rouen. A later telegram gave a list of the dead, in which was the name of his wife; and three days after I received from him the most pitiful letter that it has ever been my misfortune to read. The whole wounded soul of the man seemed laid bare upon the paper; the simplicity of his words was so touching and so expressive of his agony, that I could scarce trust myself to go through the long pages over which he let his sorrow flow. Yet one paragraph re- mained long in my mind, for it was one that recalled the necklace of green diamonds, and it was so astonish- ing that I did not doubt that Brewer was, for the time at any rate, on the high road to madness. "I have put them round her dear neck," he said, "and they shall cling always to her in her long sleep."

At the end of the month he wrote again, mentioning that, despite my sharp remonstrance, he had seen the jewels buried with her, and that his heart was broken. He said that he thought of coming to stay with me, and of retiring from business; but went on in the next para- graph to confess his inability to leave the city in which she was buried, and the places which kept her memory so sharply before him. I wrote an answer, advising

D

him to plunge into work as an antidote to grief, and had posted it but an hour when the mystery of the green diamond necklace began.

The circumstances were these. My clerk had left with the letters, and I was sitting at my table examining a few unusually large cat's-eyes which had been offered to me that morning. I heard the shop door open, and saw from the small window near my desk a man in

"'AND THEY SHALL CLING ALWAYS TO HER IN HER LONG SLEEP.'"

a fur coat, who seemed in something of a hurry when he went to the counter. Three minutes afterwards, Michel came up to me breathlessly and stammering. He carried in his hand the identical necklace which I had made for my friend Brewer, and which he had buried with his wife, as his letter said, not a month before. My amazement at the sight of it was so great that for many minutes I sat clasping and unclasping the snap of the trinket, and reading again that strange inscription, *major lex amor est nobis*, which had caused me so much amusement when I had first ordered it to be cut. Then I asked Michel,—

"Who brought this?"

"A man in the shop below—the agent of Green & Sons, who have been offered it by a customer at Dieppe."

"Have they put a price upon it?"

"They ask one thousand five hundred pounds for it."

"Oh, five hundred less than we sold it for; that is curious. Ask the man if he will leave it on approval for a week?"

"I have put the question already. His people are quite willing."

"Then write out a receipt."

He went away to do so, still fumbling and amazed. The thing was so astounding to one who knew the whole of the circumstances, as I did, that I told him nothing more, but examined the necklace minutely at least half a dozen times. Was it possible that there could be two sets of matching green diamonds, two infatuated lovers who had chosen the same pattern of ornament, the same strange inscription, and the same tint of stones? Such a thing was out of the question. Either Brewer had made a mistake when he said that the necklace had been buried with his wife—a theory which presupposed his return to his normal common sense—or some scoundrel had stolen it from her coffin. I determined to wire to him at once, and had written out a message when the second mystery in the history of the trinket began to unfold itself. It came to me in the form of a cablegram from Brewer himself, who asked me to go to him at Paris without delay, as something which troubled him beyond description had happened since he wrote to me.

I need not say that at the time when I received this telegram I had no idea that a second mystery had engendered it. I believed that Brewer had discovered the loss of the necklace, and had sent for me to trace the thieves. This task I entered upon very willingly; and when I had instructed Michel to ask Green & Co.— with whom we did a large business—to give me as a special and private favour the real name of the seller of the necklace, I took the eight o'clock train from Victoria; and was in Paris at dawn on the following morning. Early as it was, Brewer waited for me at the Gare du Nord, and greeted me with a welcome which was almost hysterical in its effusiveness. This I could not return, for the shock of the sight of him was enough to make any man voiceless. He had aged in look twenty years in as many months. His clothes hung in folds upon a figure that had once been the figure of a robust and finely built man; his face was wan and colourless; there were hollows above his temples, and furrows as of great age in the cheeks, which erstwhile shone with all the healthy colouring that physical vigour can give. His aspect, indeed, was pitiable; but I made a great effort to convince him that I had not noticed it, and said cheerily,—

"Well, and how is my old friend?"

"I am a widower," he answered; and there was more pathos in the simple remark than in any lament I ever heard from him. It was quite evident that his one grief still reigned in his thoughts; and I made no other attempt to conquer it.

"You have important news, or you would not have summoned me from London," I said, as we left the

station in a fiacre. "Won't you give me an idea of it
now?"

"When we reach my place I will tell you everything
and show you everything. It's very kind of you to
come, very kind indeed; but I'd sooner speak of such
things at my own house."

"You are still at Villemomble?"

"Yes; but I have an apartment by the Rue de Morny,
and am staying there now; the old home is not the same.
She is dead, you know."

I thought this remark very strange, and his manner
of giving it no less curious. He nodded his head gravely,
and continued to nod it, repeating the words and holding
my hand like some great schoolboy who feared to be
alone. He was scarcely better when we arrived at his
lodging, and he took me to a luxurious apartment which
was well worthy of his consummate taste; but the
moment he had shut the outer door his manner changed,
becoming quick, interested, and distinctly nervous.

"Bernard," he said, "I brought you to Paris because
the strangest thing possible has happened. You remember the necklace of green diamonds I gave my poor wife,
and buried with her?"

"Am I likely to forget that folly?" I asked.

"Well," he continued, "it was stolen from her grave
in the little cemetery near Raincy——"

"I know that," said I.

"You know it!" he cried, looking up aghast. "How
could you know it?"

"Because it was offered to me yesterday."

"Good God!" he exclaimed, "offered to you yesterday!
But it could not have been, for my servant bought it in a
shabby jeweller's near the Rue St. Lazarre! Look for
yourself, and say what do you call that?"

He had unlocked a small safe as he spoke, and he threw a jewel case upon the table. I opened it quickly, and it was then my turn to call out as he had done a moment before. The case contained a second necklace of green diamonds exactly resembling the one I had made, and had then in my pocket; and it bore even the memorable inscription—*major lex amor est nobis.*

When I made this discovery there seemed something so uncanny and terrible about it that the beads of perspiration stood on my forehead, and my hand shook until I nearly dropped the case.

"Frank," I said, "there's deeper work here than you think; this is the necklace which you believe you buried with your wife; well, what is this one, then, that I have in my pocket?"

I opened the second case and laid the jewels side by side. You could not have told one bauble from the other unless you had possessed such an eye as mine, which will fidget over a sham diamond when it is yet a yard away. He had no doubt that they were identical; and when he saw them together, he began to cry like a frightened woman.

"What does it mean?" he asked. "Have they robbed my wife's grave? My God!—two necklaces alike down to the very engraving. Who has done it? Who could do such a thing with a woman who never harmed a living soul? Bernard, if I spent every shilling I possess, I will get to the bottom of this thing! Oh, my wife, my wife——"

His distress would have moved an adamantine heart, and was not a thing to cavil at. The mystery, which had completely unnerved him, had fascinated me so strangely that I determined not to leave Paris until the last line of its solution was written. The robbery of the grave I could quite understand, but that there should be two necklaces, one of them with real stones and the other with imitation, was a fact before which my imagination reeled. As for him, he continued to sit in his arm-chair, and to fret like a child; and there I left him while I went to consult the first detective I could run against.

The difficulties in getting at the police of Paris are proverbial. The officials there hold it such an impertinence for a mere civilian to inform them of anything at all, that the unfortunate pursuer of the criminal comes at last to believe himself guilty of some crime. I put up with some hours badgering at the nearest bureau, and then having no French but that which is fit for publication, I returned to the Rue de Morny, getting on the way some glimmer of a plan into my head. I found Brewer in the same wandering state as I had left him; and although he listened when I spoke, I felt sure that his mind was in that infantile condition which can neither beget a plan nor realize one. For himself, he had a single idea; and upon that he harped *usque ad nauseam.*

"I must send for Jules," he kept muttering; "Jules knew her well; he was one of her oldest friends; he would help me in a case like this, I feel sure. He always told her that green diamonds were unlucky; I was insane to touch the things, positively insane. Jules will come at once, and I will tell him everything, and he will explain things we do not understand. Perhaps you will send a letter to him now; Robert is in the kitchen and he will take it."

"I will send a note with pleasure if you think this man can help us; but who is he, and why have I not heard of him before?"

"You must have heard of him," he answered testily; "he was always with us when she lived—always."

"Do you see him often now?"

"Yes, often; he was here a week ago; that is his photograph on the cabinet there."

The picture was that of a finely built but very typical Frenchman, a man with a pointed, well-brushed beard, and a neatly curled moustache. The head was not striking, being cramped above the eyes and bulging behind the ears; but the smile was very pleasant, and the general effect one of geniality. I examined the photograph, and then asked casually,—

"What is this M. Jules? you don't tell me the rest of his name."

"Jules Galimard. I must have mentioned him to you. He is the editor, or something, of *Paris et Londres.* We will write for him now, and he will come over at once."

I sent the letter to please him, asking the man to come across on important business, and then told him of my plan.

"The first thing to do," said I, "is to go to Raincy, and to ascertain if the grave of your wife has been tampered with—and when. If you will stay here and nurse yourself, I will do that at once?"

He seemed to think over the proposition for some minutes; and when he answered me he was calmer.

"I will come with you," he said; "if— if any one is to look upon her face again, it shall be me."

I could see that a terrible love gave him strength even for such an ordeal as this. He began to be meaningly and even alarmingly calm; and when we set out for Raincy he betrayed no emotion whatever. I will not describe anything but the result of that never-to-be-forgotten mission, although the scene haunts my memory

to this day. Suffice it to say that we found indisputable
evidence of a raid upon the vault; and discovered that
the necklace had been torn from the body of the woman.
When nothing more was to be learnt, I took my friend
back to Paris. There I found a letter from the office of
Paris et Londres saying that Galimard was at Dieppe
but would be with us in the evening.

The mystery had now taken such hold of me that I
could not rest. Brewer, whose calm was rather dangerous than re-assuring, seemed strangely lethargic when
he reached his rooms, and began to doze in his arm-
chair. This was the best thing he could have done; but
I had no intention of dozing myself; and when I had
wormed from him the address of the shop where the
sham necklace had been purchased—it proved to be in
the Rue Stockholm—I took a fiacre at once and left him
to his dreaming. The place was a poor one, though the
taste of a Frenchman was apparent in the display and
arrangement of the few jewels, bronzes, and pictures
which were the stock-in-trade of the dealer. He himself
was a lifeless creature, who listened to me with great
patience, and appeared to be completely astounded when
I told him that I desired to have an interview with the
vendor of the necklace and the green diamonds.

" You could not have come at a more fortunate
moment," said he, " the stones were pretty, I confess
and I fear to have sold them for much less than they
were worth; but my client will be here in half an hour
for his money, and if you come at that time you can
meet him."

This was positive and altogether unlooked-for luck. I
spent the thirty minutes' interval in a neighbouring
café, and was back at his shop as the clocks were striking
seven. His customer was already there; a man short

and thick in figure, with a characteristic French low hat
stuck on the side of his head; and an old black cutaway
coat which was conspicuously English. He wore
gaiters, too—a strange sight in Paris; and carried
under his arm a rattan cane which was quite ridiculously short. When he turned his head I saw that his
hair was cropped quite close, and that he had a great
scar down one side of his face, which gave him a
hideous appearance. Yet he could not have been
twenty-five years of age; and he was one of the gayest
customers I have ever met.

"Oh," he said, looking me up and down critically, and
with a perky cock of his head, "you're the cove that
wants to speak to me about the sparklers, are you? and
a damned well-dressed cove, too. I thought you were
one of these French hogs."

"I wanted to have a chat about such wonderful
imitations," I said, "and am English like yourself."

At this he raked up the gold which the old dealer had
placed upon the counter for him and went to the door
rapidly, where he stood with his hands upon his hips,
and a wondrous knowing smile in his bit of an eye.

"You're a pretty nark, ain't you?" he said, "a fine
slap-up Piccadilly thick-un, s' help me blazes; and you
ain't got no bracelets in your pockets, and there ain't
no more of you round the corner. Oh, hell! but this is
funny!"

"I am quite alone," I said quickly, seeing that the
game was nearly lost, "and if you tell me what I want
to know, I will give you as much money as you have in
your hand there, and you have my word that you shall
go quite free."

"Your word!" he replied, looking more knowing
than ever; "that's a ripping fine Bank of Engraving

"'DO YOU FEEL IT? IT'S A COLT, AIN'T IT?'"

to go on bail on, ain't it? Who are you, and how's your family?"

"Let's stroll down the street, any way you like," said I, "and talk of it. Choose your own course, and then you will be sure that I am alone."

He looked at me for a minute, walking slowly. Then suddenly he stopped abruptly, and put his hand upon a pocket at his waist.

"Guv'ner," he said, "lay your fingers on that; do you feel it? it's a Colt, ain't it? Well, if you want to get me in on the bow, I tell you I'll go the whole hog, so you know."

"I assure you again that I have no intention of troubling you with anything but a few questions; and I give you my word that anything you tell me shall not be used against you afterwards. It's the other man we want to catch--the man who took the green diamonds which were not shams."

This thought was quite an inspiration. He considered it for a moment, standing still under the lamp; but at last he stamped his foot and whistled, saying,--

"You want him, do you? well, so do I; and if I could punch his head I'd walk a mile to do it. You come to my room, guv'ner, and I'll take my chance of the rest."

The way lay past the Chapel of the Trinity, and so through many narrow streets to one which seemed the centre of a particularly dark and uninviting neighbourhood. The man, who told me in quite an affable mood that his name was Bob Williams, and that he hoped to run against me at Auteuil, had a miserable apartment on the "third" of a house in this dingy street; and there he took me, offering me half-a-tumbler of neat whisky, which, he went on to explain, would "knock flies" out of me. For himself, he sat upon a low bed

and smoked a clay pipe, while I had an arm-chair, lacking springs; and one of my cigars for obvious reasons.
When we were thus accommodated he opened the ball,
being no longer nervous or hesitating.

"Well, old chap,"—I was that already to him—"what
can I tell you, and what do you know?"

"I know this much," said I; "last month the grave
of Madame Brewer at Raincy was rifled. The man who
did it stole a necklace of green diamonds, real or sham,
but the latter, I am thinking."

"As true as gospel—I was the man who took them,
and they were sham, and be damned to them!"

"Well, you're a pretty ruffian," I said. "But what I
want to know is, how did you come to find out that the
stones were there, and who was the man who got the
real necklace I made for Madame Brewer only a few
months ago?"

"Oh, that's what you want to know, is it? Well, it's
worth something, that is; I don't know that he ain't a
pard of mine; and about no other necklace I ain't heard
nothing. You know a blarmed sight too much, it seems
to me, guv'ner."

"That may be," said I, "but you can add to what I
know, and it might be worth fifty pounds to you."

"On the cushion?"

"I don't understand."

"Well, on that table then?"

"Scarcely. Twenty-five now, and twenty-five when
I find that you have told me the truth."

"Let's see the shiners."

I counted out the money on to the bed—five English
bank notes, which he eyed suspiciously.

"May, his mark," he said, thumbing the paper.
"Well, as I'm shifting for Newmarket to-morrow that's

not much odds, if you're not shoving the queer on me."

" Do you think they're bad?"

" I'll tell you in a moment; i broken, e broken, water-mark right; guv'ner, I'll put up with 'em. Now, what do you want to know?"

"I want to know how you came to learn that the stones were in Madame Brewer's grave?"

" A straight question. Well, I was told by a pal."

" Is he here in Paris?"

" He ought to be; he told me his name was Mougat, but I found out that it ain't. He is a chap that writes for the papers and runs that rag with the rum pictures in it; what do you call it, Paris and something or other?"

" *Paris et Londres*," I ventured at hazard.

" Ay, that's the thing; I don't read much of the lingo myself, but I gave him tips at Longchamps last month, and we came back in a dog-cart together. It was then that he put me on to the stones and planted me with a false name."

" What did he say?"

" Said that some mad cove at Raincy had buried a necklace worth two thousand pounds with his wife, and that the dullest chap out could get into the vault and lift it. I'd had a bad day, and was almost stony. He kept harping on the thing so, suggesting that a man could get to America with five thousand in his pocket, and no one be a penny the wiser or a penny the worse, that I went off that night and did it, and got a fine heap for my pains. That's what I call a mouldy pal—a pal I wouldn't make a doormat of."

" And you sold the booty to the old Frenchman in the Rue de Stockholm?"

"Exactly! he gave me a tenner for it, and I'm cross-
ing to England to-night. No place like the old shop,
guv'ner, when the French hogs are sniffing about you.
I guess there's a few of them will want me in Parry in
a day or two; and that reminds me, you can do the
noble if you like, and send the other chips to the
Elephant Hotel at Cambridge last post to-morrow."

I told him that I would, and left. You may ask why
I had any truck with such a complete blackguard, but the
answer is obvious: I had guessed from the first that there
was something in the mystery of the green diamonds
which would not bear exposure from Brewer's point of
view, and his tale confirmed the opinion. I had learnt from
it two obvious facts: one that Jules Galimard was anything but the friend of my friend; the other, that this
man knew perfectly well that a sham diamond necklace
was buried with Madame Brewer. It came to me then,
as in a flash, that he, and he alone, must have stolen, or
at least have come into possession of, the real necklace
which I had made.

How to undeceive the good soul who had entrusted me
with his case was the remaining difficulty. He had
loved this woman so; and yet instinct suggested to me
that she had been unworthy of his deep affection. That
she had been untrue to him I did not know. Galimard
might have stolen the jewels from her, and have re-
placed them with a false set; on the other hand, she
might have been a party to the fraud. What, then,
should I say, or how much should I dare with the great
responsibility before me of crushing a man whose heart
was already broken?

With such thoughts I re-entered the apartment in the
Rue de Morny. As I did so, the servant put a telegram
into my hand, and told me that M. Jules Galimard was

with his master. Fate, however, seemed to have given the man another chance, for the cipher said,—

"Green and Co. in error, they should have sent the stones only; necklace not for sale; client's name unknown, acting for Paris agents."

I walked into the room with this message in my pocket; and when Brewer saw me he jumped up with delight, and introduced me to a well-dressed Frenchman who had the red rosette in the buttonhole of his faultless frock-coat, and who showed a row of admirable teeth when he smiled to greet me.

"Here is Jules," said Brewer, "my friend I have spoken of, M. Jules Galimard; he has come to help us, as I said he would; there is no one whose advice I would sooner take in this horrible matter."

I bowed stiffly to the man, and seated myself on the opposite side of the table to him. As they seemed to wait for me to speak, I took up the question at once.

"Well," I said, speaking to Brewer; but turning round to look at his friend, as I uttered the words, "I have found out who sold the sham necklace to the man in the Rue de Stockholm; the rogue is a racing tout named Bob Williams."

Galimard turned right round in his chair at this, and put his elbows on the table. Brewer said, "God bless me, what a scamp!"

"And," I continued, "the extraordinary part of the affair is that this scoundrel was put up to the business by a man he met at Longchamps last month. It is obvious that this man stole the real necklace, and now desired all traces of his handiwork to be removed from Madame Brewer's coffin. I have his name," with which direct remark I looked hard at the fellow, and he rose straight up from his chair and clutched at the back of en

'e

iT

l

i the
ed to
e.
rning
ls, "I
man
rout

nd

li

&
of

"HE STRUCK THE RASCAL WHO TOLD HIM THE TALE FULL IN
THE MOUTH WITH HIS CLENCHED FIST."

it with his hand. For a moment he seemed speechless; but when he found his tongue, he threw away, with dreadful maladroitness, the opening I had given him.

"Madame gave me the jewels," he blurted out, "that I will swear before any court."

The situation was truly terrible, the man standing gripping his chair, Brewer staring at both of us as at lunatics.

"What do you say? What's that?" he cried; and the assertion was repeated.

"I am no thief!" cried the man, drawing himself up in a way that was grotesquely proud, "she gave me the jewels, your wife, a week after you gave them to her. I had a false set made so that you should not miss them; here is her letter in which she acknowledges the receipt of them."

The old man—for he was an old man then in speech, in look, and in the fearful convulsions of his face—sprung from his chair, and struck the rascal who told him the tale full in the mouth with his clenched fist. The fellow rolled backwards, striking his head against the iron of the fender; and lay insensible for many minutes. During that time I called a cab, and when he was capable of being moved, sent him away in it. I saw clearly that for Brewer's sake the matter must be hushed at once, blocked out as a page in a life which had been false in its every line. Nor did I pay any attention to Galimard's raving threat that his friends should call upon me in half an hour; but went upstairs again to find the best soul that ever lived sitting over the fire which had been lighted for him, and chattering with the cackle of the insane. He had the letter, which Galimard had thrown down, in his hands, and he read it aloud with hysterical laughter and awful emphasis.

I tried to speak to him, to reason with him, to persuade him. He heard nothing I said, but continued to chuckle and to chatter in a way that made my blood run cold. Then suddenly he became very calm, sitting bolt upright in his chair, with the letter clutched tightly in his right hand; and I saw that tears were rolling down his cheeks.

An hour later the friends of M. Jules Galimard called. They entered the room noisily, but I hushed them, for the man was dead!

THE COMEDY OF THE JEWELLED LINKS

THE COMEDY OF THE JEWELLED LINKS

I DO not know if there be any drug in the Pharma-copœia, or any clearly defined medical treatment, which may ever hope to grapple effectively with the strange disease of jewel-hunger, but if there be not, I have much pleasure in recommending this most singular ill to the notice of a rising generation of physicans. That it is a branch of that mystery of mysteries, *la névrose*, I have no manner of doubt, for I have seen it in all its forms—a malignant growth which makes night of the lives it plays upon; and flourishes to exceeding profit down in the very heart of tragedies. For the matter of that, the flunkeys, who study in the kitchen—as the great master has told us—the characters of their governing acquaintances in the boudoir above over a quart pot and the *Police News*, get no little insight into the development of the social disaster which treads often upon the heels of jewel-hunger, as they read those extravagantly ornate reports of robbery and of mystery in which a highly moral people revels. These are but gleaners in the field—to them the inner life must remain hidden. No physican hoping to cope with the affection should turn either to gossips or to slanderers for his diagnosis. Let him get down into the caves of the trade, give his ear to the truer narrative which the jewel dealer alone can write for him, and he may hope·for material and for success. And if he be wise, he will study both the comedy and the tragedy which such an investigation will bring before him, and will by this means alone set himself up as a specialist.

It is to such a one that I would recommend perusal of the following case which I record here as one of the comedies of my note-book—a story of meanness, cupidity, and stupid cunning; I doubt if there be any philosophy of medicine which could make pretence of solving it. There were but two principal actors mentioned in the argument, and, indeed, it might fairly be called a one-part play. The chief person concerned, Lord Harningham, I had known for many years. He was a man of whom a biographer wrote " that his long and unblemished career was a credit to his county," and to whom a book on the Decalogue was inscribed as to one *sans peur et sans rèproche*. Yet they told you in the smoking-rooms that he had starved his first wife, and left his only son as the partner of a horse-coper in Melbourne, on the princely allowance of one hundred and fifty pounds per annum. His wealth, said common report, was anything from fifty thousand to a hundred thousand pounds per annum; and in his second childhood, for he was a septuagenarian when this comedy was played, he was suckled on the nourishing food of expiring leases and forfeited improvements until he seemed to exude sovereigns from every pore in his enormous body.

A meaner man never lived. All similes in converse were based upon his exploits. " As mean as old Harningham " was a phrase you heard every day at the " Bachelors." In the countless old stories they put upon him, telling how, at a tenants' lunch in Bedfordshire, he had cried, " Here's another quart of cider, and hang the expense!" how he had been seen in Farringdon Market buying his own fish; how he haggled with cabmen innumerable; how he had been stricken with a malignant fever on the day he gave away a sovereign for a shilling—there was but the echo of the general

"A MEANER MAN NEVER LIVED."

sentiment. The society prints were hilarious at the mere mention of his name. I recollect well his anger when a wag said in one of them, "It is rumoured that Lord Harningham is shortly about to give something away." He was in my office next day—a week rarely passed but what I saw him—and he laid the journal upon my table, beating it flat with his stick, and pointing at it with his ample finger as though his very touch would wither the writer.

"Please to read that," he said with forced calm but considerable emphasis, "and tell me if the scoundrel dosen't deserve to be hanged. He dares to mention my name, d'ye see! To mention *me*, and speak about my concerns. Ha! but I wish I had him under this stick!"

"Of course you don't know who wrote it," said I.

"How should I know?" he gabbled testily. "Do I go round to the taverns swilling gin-and-water with such gutter birds? Do I hobnob with all the half-starved limners in Fleet Street? Pshaw, you talk like a fool!"

I suffered his temper, for he was worth a couple of thousand a year to me. Presently he became calmer, and the humour of the thing dawned upon his dull mind.

"Ha!" he said, snuffing ferociously from the great diamond-studded box he always carried, "I shouldn't wonder if that's Master Bertie Watts—you know my nephew, eh? he owes you something, eh?—well, that's like him, and his scoundrelly impudence—the vagabond!"

"Did not I read somewhere that he was going to be married?" I remarked at hazard; but the notion tickled him immensely, and he rolled about in his chair, shaking the snuff from his box over his fur coat, and even upon my papers.

"Yes, you read it," he gasped at last, "and a fine tale too. Why, what's he got?—four hundred a year in

Whitehall, and what he can draw out of me—not much, Mr. Sutton—not much."

I had no doubt of that, but I kept my face while he went on to mutter and to chortle; and I showed him a bracelet of rubies, which he desired instantly to purchase. I had put a price of four hundred and twenty pounds upon it, meaning to accept three hundred, so that we haggled for two hours by the clock and had then done business. He took the rubies away with him, while I caused the further sum to be set against him in the ledger, where already there were so many unpaid items under his name. He owed me eight thousand pounds at the least, but I could not press the account, or should have lost him; and while I was often sore troubled for lack of the money, I knew that I should get it at his death, and so aided his jewel-hunger. This was prodigious. All the gems that I sold—watches, necklaces, tiaras, brooches, and breast-pins, were conveyed at once to the great safe in his bedroom and there immured. No one ever saw them but himself. His wives, both of whom were dead, had scarce enjoyed the possession of a barmaid's jewellery. The passion of the collector, of the hungerer after stones, alone consumed him. Of all his meanness, this was the most contemptible—this hiding of fair treasure from the light it lived upon—this gross hoarding of beautiful things for one man's selfish enjoyment.

When he left Bond Street that day, crying at my door, "So I'm going to give something away, am I?— but I ain't, Sutton, I ain't"—and walking off as though he had found satisfaction in the negative thus conveyed to me, I picked up the paper, and read again that young Bertie Watts was at last engaged to the Hon. Eva Benley, and that the wedding was to be celebrated in a month's time. Every one in town said that old Harningham would do something for Watts when the time for the marriage actually came; and it was gossip in the clubs that her people had given their consent—for they were historically poor—only upon the sincere assurance from their daughter's *fiancé* that his uncle really was very fond of him, and would present him with a handsome cheque on the wedding day. But here was the announcement of the wedding, and the old curmudgeon had just said—being readier in speech with me, perhaps, than with any one of his few acquaintances—that he did not mean to give the young people a halfpenny. It did occur to me that possibly he might have bought the ruby bracelet for the exceedingly pretty girl to whom his nephew was engaged; but in this I was mistaken, as you shall presently see; and the interest of the whole problem deepened when I learnt later on in the smoking-room of my club that the marriage was likely to be postponed, and something of a scandal to ensue. Bertie Watts, they said, was going about like a ravenous beast, seeking what financier he could devour. His opinion of his uncle was expressed in phrases of which the chief ornament was appalling curses and maledictions. He declared he would have the whip-hand of him yet, would make him pay hansomely for all the trouble he had put people to—in short, behaved like a man who was absurdly in love, regardless of that financial prudence which is so dear to the sight of parents and of guardians. Even he, however, could not foresee the strange thing about to happen to him, or the very curious opportunity which was shortly to be his.

A week passed. There was no definite announcement of any postponement of the arrangements noted by

The Hyde Park Gazette, nor did such part of society as
is represented by the tonguesters, hear that Bertie had

" HE CAME TO ME ON THE FOLLOWING MORNING FOR A DIAMOND AIGRETTE."

persuaded his uncle. The thing was a kind of deadlock
in its financial aspect, until at last the world of Bel-
gravia knew that the young lady's father, Lord Varnley,

had consented to let the wedding be, and to trust to
Harningham's better sense when the time of the accom-
plishment came.   I saw Watts one day driving with his
fiancée near the Achilles Statue, and thought that he
looked glum enough; but he came to me on the following morning for a diamond aigrette, and although he
couldn't pay for it I let him have it.

"It'll be all right in a month, Sutton," said he; "you
know the old chap's hard enough, but he can't let me
marry on nothing a year, can he now?"

I said that the thing was possible; and for his own
sake ventured to hint that it was even probable, an
opinion which he took in no good part, sucking his stick
silently for a while, and then laughing with a poor
little chuckle that seemed to come from the very top of
his head.

"Well," he exclaimed at last, "it's devilish rough on
a fellow to have a relation of that sort, isn't it?—a
positive disgrace to the family.   I wonder what the old
blackguard is going to give me for a wedding present.
Did he ask you to show him any American tickers, by
the way?   I shouldn't wonder if he presented me with
a brass clock, and Eva with a guinea set in jet—he's
mean enough."

"He bought a ruby bracelet here some days ago," I
remarked, as in parenthesis.

"Did he now?" he exclaimed in a tone of pleasure.
"I wonder if its for the girlie! but, of course, it couldn't
be.   He'd die to give away anything that once went
into his old safe.   Look here, Sutton, couldn't you
charge him an extra hundred, and go halves?   I feel
like something desperate."

I told him that that was impossible, and he went
away with the aigrette in his pocket, and a very thought-

ful expression upon his face. Before he did so, however, he had uttered the pious wish that his uncle might die of some tormenting visitation; and that he might be alive to dance on the day of the funeral. I must say that I sympathised with him, for he was a good-looking and kindly-hearted young fellow, who for many years had been led to believe that his relations would do something for him; and who was about to be grievously disappointed. Nor could I forget that he was engaged to one of the prettiest girls in town—and for her sake enjoyed a kind of reflected sympathy which was sincere enough on the part of every man who knew him,

The date of the wedding was now fixed, being the 21st of January, to be well ahead of Lent. I saw Watts very frequently during the following ten days, he coming with expectant persistency to ask me if his uncle had yet bought him anything; and remaining disappointed almost to the very eve of his marriage. In fact, the wedding was to take place on the Wednesday, and it was only on the previous Monday that Lord Harningham ascended my stairs puffing and blowing, and in a shocking temper, to make his purchase of a present.

"Sutton," he said, "this is the greatest tomfoolery on earth—that young rascal is going to get married after all, and I suppose I'll have to give him something."

"You can scarce do less," I said with a smile.

"Of course I can do less," he replied garrulously. "I can give him nothing at all, d'ye see; not a brass halfpenny. Look at the ass, maudling about the first pretty face he sees over a dinner table when he might marry money twenty times for the asking of it. Did I make such a fool of myself when I was his age?"

I assured him that he did nothing of the sort.

"Then what's he want to do it for? Thinks he's going to get something out of me, perhaps—out of *me*, but he ain't—not sixpence; not if they hadn't enough to get to the station with. Ha, ha! I'm not such a spendthrift as I look."

He talked in this strain for some while, and then fell to haggling over a gift. He told me that the custom of giving wedding presents was the insane fashion of an insane age; that he consented to follow it only in view of the fuss that society would make if his card did not lie on Lord Varnley's table when the other presents were shown. In this bargaining he displayed a meanness which was triumphant even for him. I must have shown him quite a hundred rings, pins, and watches, of all values, from fifty pounds to five hundred, before he could in any way make up his mind; and he did not cease to rebuke me for that which he called my preposterously extravagant insinuation. "Fifty sovereigns! a hundred sovereigns!" he kept exclaiming; "why, man alive, do you think I'm made of money? Show me something cheap, something that five pounds will buy, d'ye see? any bit of stuff's good enough for a jackanapes like that."

"But not for your card on Lord Varnley's table."

"Why, what do you mean?"

"People who are uncharitable, you know, might say that it was a curiously insufficient present."

"D'ye think they'd say that?"

"I am sure they would."

"Pshaw!—so am I; that comes of being thought a rich man when you're as poor as a parson. I'm quite a poor man, you know, Sutton."

I listened to him patiently, and in the end persuaded him to buy Watts an exquisite set of jewelled links.

These had a fine diamond in each of them, but their greatest ornament was the superb enamelling, worthy of Jean Toutin or Petitot, with which all the gold was covered. I asked one hundred and fifty pounds for these remarkable ornaments; and the old man, struck,

"I MUST HAVE SHOWN HIM QUITE A HUNDRED RINGS, PINS, AND WATCHES."

like the artist he was, with the perfection of the workmanship, fixed his greedy eyes upon them, and was persuaded. He protested that they were too good, far too good, for such a worthless ingrate as his nephew, and that he ought to keep them in his own collection; but at

F

last he ordered me to send them, with his card, to Lord Varnley's town house, and went away chafing at his own generosity, and, as he avowed, at his stupidity.

I saw no more of him for a week. The wedding had been celebrated, and Master Bertie Watts had conveyed away quietly to Folkestone as pretty an English girl as ever flourished in the glare of the West. Lord and Lady Varnley shut up their house during the week after the marriage, having sent the very numerous wedding presents to their bankers; and society would have forgotten the whole business if it had not paused to discuss the important question—How were the young couple to exist in the future on the paltry income of four or five hundred pounds a year? One half of the world may not know how the other half lives, but that is not for lack of effort on its part to find out. It was a matter of club-room news that old Lord Harningham had not relented —and, beyond what his nephew called "those twopenny-half-penny sleeve links," had not given him a penny. How then, said this same charitable world, will these silly children keep up their position in town when they return from the second-rate hotel they are now staying in at Folkestone?

Curiously enough, I was able myself to answer that question in three days' time—though at the moment I was as ignorant as any of them. The matter came about in this way. On the very morning that Lord Varnley went to Paris, it was known through the daily papers that there had been a robbery at his house in Cork Street, of a green velvet case, containing a crescent of pearls, turquoises, and diamonds. This was a present from one of the Embassies to his daughter, and must, said the reports, have been abstracted from the house during the press and the confusion of the reception. Later in the afternoon I received an advice from Scotland Yard cautioning me against the purchase of such a gem, and inviting immediate communication if it were offered to me. The theft of wedding presents is so common that I gave little heed to the matter; and was already immersed in other business when Lord Harningham was announced. He seemed rather fidgety in his manner, I thought, and hummed and hawed considerably before he would explain his mission.

"It's about those links I gave my nephew," he said at last. "They're far too good for him, Sutton—and they're too pretty. I never saw better work in my life, and must have been a fool when I let them go out of my possession—d'ye see?"

"Well, but you can't get them back now?" I remarked with a smile.

He took snuff vigorously at my reply, and then said,—

"Man, you're wrong, I've got them in my pocket."

I must have expressed my astonishment in my look, for he went on quickly,—

"Yes, here in the green case as you sold them. Do I surprise you, eh? Well, I'm going to give Master Bertie a bit of a cheque and to keep these things; but one of the stones is off colour—I noticed it at the wedding—and I must have a new one in, d'ye see?"

"I thought that you had already handed them over," I interrupted, quite disregarding his last request.

"So I did, so I did; but a man can take his own back again, can't he? Well, when I saw them at the house, I concluded it was ridiculous to give a boy like that such treasures, and so——"

"You spoke to him?"

"Hem—that is, of course, man. Pshaw! You're too

inquisitive for a jeweller: you ought to have been a lady's maid."

" Have you brought them with you now ? "

" What should I be here for if I hadn't ? "

He laid upon my table a green velvet case, of the exact size, colour, and shape of that which had contained the links ; but when I opened it I gave a start, and put it down quickly. The case held a crescent of pearls, turquoises, and diamonds, which answered exactly to the description of the one stolen from Lord Varnley's house on the day of his daughter's wedding.

" There's some mistake here," said I, " you've evidently left the links at home," with which remark I put the jewels under his very nose for him to see. He looked at them for a moment, the whole of his flabby face wrinkling and reddening ; then he seemed almost to choke, and the veins in his forehead swelled until they were as blue threads upon an ashen and colourless countenance.

" Good God ! " he ejaculated, "I've taken the wrong case."

" Your nephew gave it you, no doubt, but he must have forgotten it, for he's advertised the loss of this crescent at Scotland Yard, and there are detectives now trying to find it. I am cautioned not to purchase it," I said with a laugh.

The effect of these words upon him was so curious that for some moments I thought he had spasm of the heart. Starting up in the chair, with wild eyes, and hands clutching at the arms to rest upon them, he made several attempts to speak, but not a word came from his lips. I endeavoured to help him with his difficulty, but it was to little purpose.

" It seems to me, Lord Harningham," I suggested,

" that you have only to write a line of explanation to your nephew—and there's an end of the matter."

" You think so ? " he cried eagerly.

" Why not," said I, " since he returned the jewels to you ? "

" But he didn't," he interrupted, cringing in the chair at this confession of a lie ; " he didn't ; and he'd prosecute me ; he hates me, and this is his opportunity, d'ye see ? "

" Do you mean to say," I exclaimed, beginning to understand the situation, " that you took the case without his permission ? "

" Yes, yes," he mumbled, " they were so beautiful, such work ! You know what work they were. I saw them at the wedding, and was sure that I should not have parted with them. I meant to send him a cheque against them—and when no one was looking I put what I thought was the case into my pocket, but it was the wrong one. God help me, Sutton, what shall I do ? "

Now it seemed to me that this was one of the most delightful comedies I had ever assisted at. Technically, Lord Harningham was a thief, and undoubtedly Bertie Watts could have prosecuted him had he chosen, though the probability of his getting a conviction was small. But it was very evident to me that here was the boy's opportunity, and that in the interest of his pretty wife I should make the best of it. With this intent, I played my first card with necessary boldness.

" Undoubtedly the case is very serious for you," said I, apparently with sympathy, " and it is made the more serious from the strange relations existing between your nephew and yourself. You know the law, I doubt not, as well as I do ; and that once a prosecu-

tion has been initiated at Scotland Yard it is impossible
to withdraw without a trial.   Mr. Watts might get into
serious trouble for compounding a felony ; and I might
suffer with him as one in the conspiracy.   But I tell you
what I will do; I'll write to him to-night and sound
him.   Meanwhile, let me advise you to keep out of
the way, for I can't disguise the fact that you might be
arrested."

He gave a great scream at this, and the perspiration
rolled from him, falling in great drops upon the carpet.
"Oh, Lord!" he kept muttering, "oh, that I should
have been such a consummate fool!—oh, Heaven help
me! To think of it—and what it will cost, I could cry,
Sutton—cry like a child."

I calmed him with difficulty, and led him down the
back stairs to a cab with a positive assurance that I
would not communicate with Scotland Yard.   Then I
wrote to Folkstone a letter, the precise contents of which
are immaterial, but the response to which was in the form
of a telegram worded as follows :—

"Am inexpressibly shocked and pained, but the law
must take its course."

I put this into my pocket without any delay and went
over to Harningham's house in Park Lane. He had
been up all night, they told me, and the doctor had just
left him; but I found him suffering only from an ener-
vating fear, and white as the cloth on the breakfast
table before him.

"Well," he said, "what is it, what does he say? Will
he prosecute me?"

I handed him the telegram for answer, and I thought
he would have swooned. He did not know that I had in
my pocket another letter from his nephew, in which
Master Bertie informed me that I was the "best chap in

the world," and I saw no reason to mention this. Indeed, I listened with infinite gravity when the old man told me that he was irretrievably ruined, and that his name would stand in all the clubs as that of a common thief. Jewel-hunger plainly accounted for everything he had done; but it was not to my end to console him, and I said in a severe and sufficiently melancholy voice,—

"Lord Harningham, there is only one thing to do, and for your sake I will make myself a criminal participator in the conspiracy. You must go to Folkstone with me this afternoon, and take your cheque book with you."

The groan he gave at this would have moved a man of iron. I saw tears standing in his eyes, and his hand shook when I left him so that he could scarce put it into mine. Yet he came to the station to meet me in the afternoon, and by six o'clock we were in Folkstone at a shabby second-rate hotel, called "The Cock and Lobster," inquiring for the bride and bridegroom. Mr. and Mrs. Watts, they said, were out on the parade; but we went to look for them, and surprised them coming from the Lees, as handsome a couple as you could look upon. She, a pretty, brown-haired English girl, her tresses tossed over her large eyes by the sharp wind that swept in from the sea, was close under the arm of her husband, who, at that stage, fearing to lose her touch, seemed engaged in the impossible attempt to cover her entirely with one of his arms. And in this pursuit privacy came to his aid, for the breeze was fresh from the Channel at the beginning of night, banishing all loiterers but those loitering in love; and the lamps flickered and went low in the gusts as though fearing to illumine the roses upon the cheeks of a bride.

When Master Bertie saw us he became as sedate as a

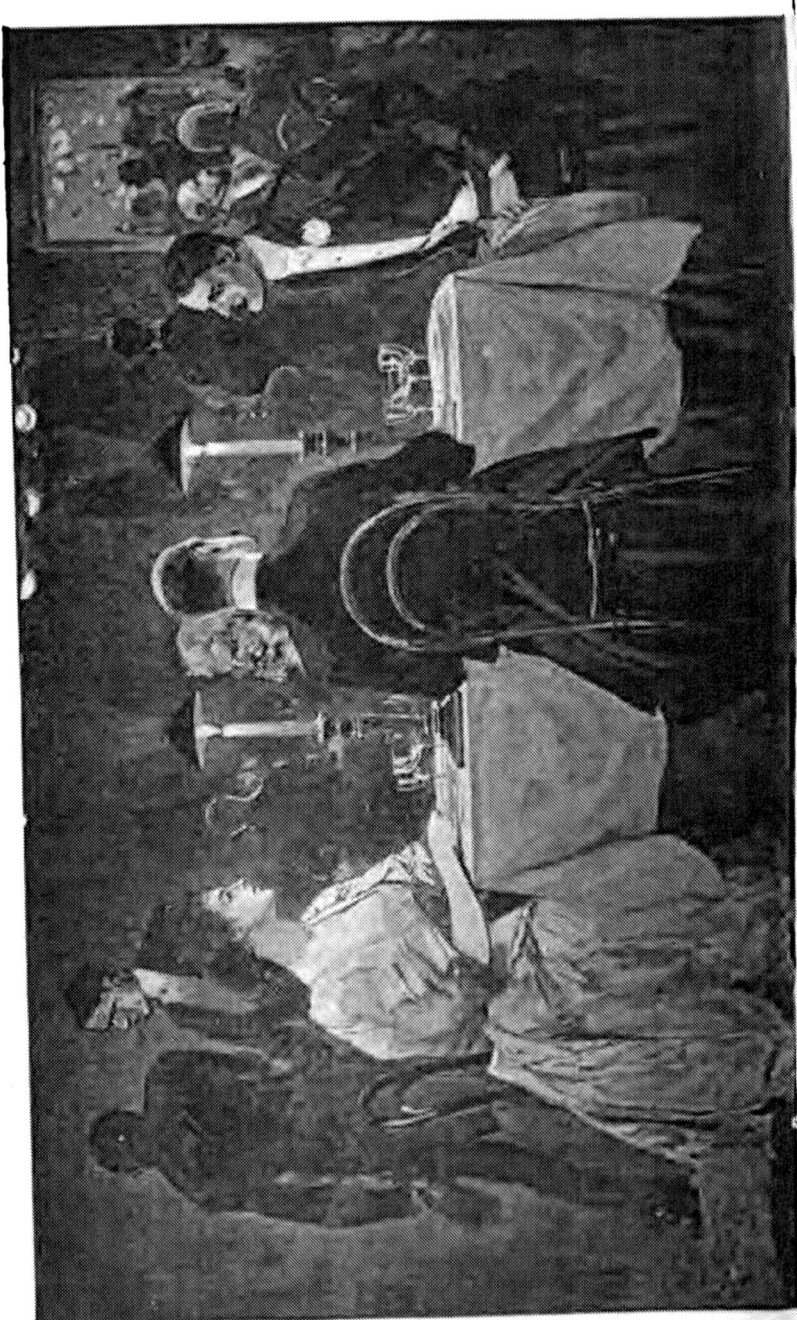

"IN AN HOUR WE WERE SITTING DOWN"

Methodist minister, and, commanding a solemn tone, acted the part to perfection.

"Uncle," he said, "I would never have believed it of you. But this is too serious a matter to mention here; let us go to the hotel."

"'IF YOU PAID MY BILL—GAVE ME, SAY, EIGHT THOUSAND POUNDS ON ACCOUNT—I BELIEVE MY MIND WOULD BE QUITE OBLIVIOUS TO THE EVENTS OF LAST NIGHT.'"

We returned in silence, but directly we were in the hall the young man called for his bill, and speaking almost in a boisterous tone, cried,—

"We're going to change our quarters, uncle, and will begin by moving to the best hotel in the place. That poor girl is moped to death here, and now you're going to pay for our honeymoon—cost doesn't matter, does it, old man?"

The old man concerned started at this, his mouth wide open with the surprise of it.

"What's that?" he muttered. "What're you going to do?" But I whispered to him to be silent, and in an hour we were sitting down to a superb dinner—which he did not touch, by the bye—in the great saloon of the biggest hotel in the place. During the meal the bride, who scarce seemed able to do anything else than look at her husband, made few remarks, but Watts and I talked freely, quite ignoring the old man; and it was not until we were in the private room that the negotiations began.

There is no need to describe them. They lasted until midnight, at which hour the nephew of Lord Harningham had five hundred pounds in his pocket, and an allowance of five hundred a year. From the moment of assenting to these conditions until we entered the train next morning the old man never opened his lips, but he kissed the bride at the door of the hotel, and colour came again to his cheeks at the warmth of her lips. When at last we were alone in the carriage he gave a great sigh of relief and said,—

"Sutton, thank God that's over!"

"Nearly over, my lord," I replied with emphasis.

"What do you mean?" he cried. "Do you think that any one will get to hear of it? Why, man, what have I half-ruined myself for?"

"To keep your nephew quiet," I suggested pleasantly.

"And who else knows anything when he's settled with?" he asked angrily.

"Why," said I quite calmly, "you and I, perhaps."

He looked at me as though his glance was all-consuming and would wither me, but I met him with a placid smile and continued,—

"It seems to me that I want what Mr. Stevenson calls 'a good memory for forgetting.' Do you know, Lord Harningham, that if you paid my bill—gave me, say, eight thousand pounds on account, I believe my mind would be quite oblivious to the events of last night."

The shot struck home—in the very centre of my target. He thought over it for some while, and spoke but once between Sevenoaks and Charing Cross. His remark was more forcible than convincing, for he exclaimed suddenly, and *a propos* of nothing in particular, "Sutton, to blazes with all jewels!" Then he subsided, and came with me quietly to my rooms, where he wrote a cheque for eight thousand pounds and signed it with considerable firmness. The ink was hardly dry, however, before he dropped heavily upon the carpet, and lay prone in a fit.

The shock of parting with so much money had been too much for him. He is now in Maderia seeking a climate.

TREASURE OF WHITE CREEK

TREASURE OF WHITE CREEK

SHE was the daughter of Colonel Kershaw Klein, and he was worth a million, as the society papers said. I had danced with her for the first time in the ball-room of the magnificent house her father had rented in Grosvenor Crescent, on the occasion of her coming of age; and I agreed with the men that she was beyond criticism, an exquisite vision of dark and matured girl-hood, so incomparably fascinating that you forget in her company some of her bluntness in speech, and set down the voluptuousness of her glance and mien to the southern luxuriance amidst which she had been reared, and to those "other" notions which prevail in Chili, the land of fleeting republics.

Some part of this perhaps unnecessary adulation may have been due to the fact that I had helped in the production of her perfect picture on the night of which I am speaking. The commercial element will intrude at such times; and I could not help but see that she wore at least eight hundred pounds' worth of my jewels. Had the value of them been double, it would have been the same to me, for of her father's stability I had then no doubt. He had been received and made much of in the highest places, accorded the chief seats at the feasts; en-trusted—as the old ladies told you—with the most important missions by Government; and a share in the Western Hill diamond mine at South Africa was not the least substantial factor in the sum of his income. Any and every gem to which he took a fancy I had let him have readily, being assured by an important personage at the Embassy that his credit was unquestionable; and it was a pretty pleasure to me when I first met his daughter to observe how well my diamonds sat upon her, and how shapely were her arms clasped in the ruby bracelets which had been amongst the treasures of Bond Street but three months before. She was, indeed, a sunny child of the South, radiating a warming light about her, tempting you to wait long for a single press of her hand, luring you to follow the sparkle of her eyes even when she looked at you over the shoulder of a dancer who for the moment had the privilege of holding her in the entrancement of the *deux temps*. There was keen contention for her programme, but somehow I found her disposed to favour me, and danced no less than four with her, to the infinite annoyance of the many youths who eyed me angrily from their watching-ground by the door. They said that they had never seen her brighter; and I was ready to believe them, for she kept her tongue going merrily through the waltzes, and leant upon my arm in a languorous way that was completely entrancing.

At the end of the dance—the next being some new-fangled " Barn Dance " wherein men scarce put their hands upon their partners—she said that she would sit in the conservatory and eat ices; and for the first time during the long evening I found myself able to talk easily with her.

"Well," she said, when we had composed ourselves behind a huge fern, and had made a successful attack upon the *meringues glacés*, " well, this is about splendid ; don't you think so?"

MARGARET.

I said that nothing could be more delightful.

"And to think that I've never danced with you before; why, you're just perfect," she went on. "I haven't enjoyed myself right along like this since I was in Valparaiso."

"Are the Chilians such wonderful dancers then?" I asked, as she looked up at me bewitchingly.

"They just make a profession of it between the shooting times," said she; and then changing the subject quickly, she asked, "What do you think of the crystals now I've got them on?"

It is not particularly consoling to hear your rubies spoken of as crystals, but her description was accompanied by such a pretty laugh, and she opened her great black eyes so widely, that I smiled when I answered,—

"Why, they're to be envied in such a setting."

"You're the fourth man that has said the same to-night," she exclaimed, putting her glass down and tugging at her glove. "I think that Britishers learn their compliments out of copy-books; they're all presents for good girls. Let's see if you're cleverer at getting a glove on than at making pretty speeches."

The arm that she held out was gloriously white; and as every man knows, the operation of pulling on the glove of a pretty girl is apt to be prolonged. There are fingers to fit, and a little thumb to stroke daintily; while the grip upon the more substantial part of the forearm will bear repetition so long as time serves. I must have occupied myself at least five minutes with her buttons, she finding it necessary to press close to me when I did so; and the task was none the less pleasant when her rich brown hair touched my face, and her dress rustled with her long-drawn breathing. How long the process would have lasted, or what I should have said foolishly

in the end, I do not know ; but of a sudden she drew her
arm away and exclaimed,—

"Oh, I'd quite forgotten ; I wanted to ask you about
the bull's-eye."

This was her description, I may mention without
anger, of the famous White Creek Diamond, which, as
all London knows, I have had in my possession for the
last two years. Her father, who was reputed to have
some commission to buy it for a Persian, was then
negotiating with me for its purchase for the sum of one
hundred and thirty thousand pounds. He waited only,
he said, for the coming of his partner from Valparaiso,
to complete the transaction ; and it was owing to the
intimacy which the *pour parlers* brought about that I
found myself then in his house. How much his daughter knew of the business, however, I could not tell, and I
answered her question by another.

"What do you know about the bull's-eye ?"

"That you're trying to sell it to my father," she
replied, "and that he won't promise to give it to me."

"Have you asked him, then ?"

"Have I asked him—why, look at him ; isn't he ten
years older since he met you in Bond-street ?"

"He certainly seems to have something on his mind,"
said I.

"That's me ; he's got me on his mind," she remarked
flippantly ; "but I wish he'd buy the bull's-eye, and give
it to me for a wedding present."

"Oh, you're engaged," I ventured dolefully ; "you
never told me that——"

"Didn't I ?" she answered, "well, of course I am, and
here's my partner."

She went away on another man's arm ; but she left to
me a vision of dark eyes and ivory white flesh ; and her

breath still seemed to blow balmily upon my forehead.
Her partner was a young man just down from Oxford,
they told me; seemingly a simple youth, to whom the
whole sentence in conversation was as much a mystery
as the binomial theorem; but he danced rather well, and
I doubt not she suffered him for that. I watched her
through the waltz, and then, after a few words with her
father, who promised to call upon me the next day concerning White Creek treasure, I said "Good night" to
her. She gave me a glance which was more entrancing
than any word; and, although she had the habit of looking at a man as though she were dying for love of him,
I carried it away with me foolishly into the street, when
the dawn had broken with summer haze, and an exalt-
ing sweetness was in the air.

The invigorating breath of morning somewhat sobered
my thoughts; but none the less left the impression of
her beauty fermenting in my mind. I turned into Hyde
Park, where the trees were alive with song-birds, and
the glowing flowers sparkled with the silver freshness
of the dew, and set out to walk to Bayswater. In these
moments, I forgot the prosaic necessities of forms and
customs; and bethought how pleasant it would be if
some enchantment could place her at my side, a Phyllis
of Mayfair, freed from the tie of conventionality, to look
at me for all time with those eyes she had used so well
but an hour ago. I forgot her manners of speech, her
unpleasing idioms, even the discordant note that her
usually melodious voice was sometimes guilty of; forgot
all but her ripe beauty, the softness of her touch, the
alluring fascination of her way, the insurpassable play
of her mouth, the exquisite perfection of her figure.

Women's eyes make dreamers of us all; and though
I have pride in the thought that I am not a susceptible

man, I will confess without hesitation that I was as near
to being in love on that summer morning in July as was

"'I WANTED TO ASK YOU ABOUT THE BULL'S-EYE.'"

ever a professor of the single state who has come within
hail of his thirty-fifth year with his anti-feminine vow
unweakened.

At Lancaster Gate I paused a moment, leaning upon the iron rail of the drive to look back at the London veldt fresh to luxuriance in the dew showers which gave many colours in the play of sunlight. There was stillness under the trees, and the hum of the still sleeping city was hushed, though day was seeking to enter the blind-hid windows, and workmen slouched heavily to their labour. The scene was fresh enough, beautiful as many of the city's scenes are beautiful; but I had scarce time to enjoy when I saw the Oxford youth who had last danced with Margaret Klein coming striding over the grass; a masterful pipe in his mouth; and a very rough ulster wrapped round his almost vanishing shoulders. He gave me a cheery nod for greeting, and to my surprise he seated himself upon the seat beside me; and having offered me a cigar, which I took, he found his tongue so readily that I, who had heard his "haw-hawing" in the ball-room, concluded at once that it was assumed and not natural to him. And in this I was right, as the first exchange of speech with him proved.

"I've had a sharp run to catch you" said he, "for this infernal dancing takes it out of you when you're not used to it. I wanted a word with you particularly before this thing goes any further. Do you know anything of those people?"

"Why," said I, "I might ask you that question, since you made yourself so much at home there; don't you know them?"

"No, I'm hanged if I do," said he; "but, if I'm not mistaken, I shall be on very good terms with them before the season's out. You haven't sold them any jewels, have you?"

This was such an extraordinary question that I turned

upon him with an angry reply upon my lips; but the
word changed to one of amazement when I saw his face
closely in the full sunlight. It was no longer the face
of an Oxford boy, but of a man of my own age at the
least.

"Whew!" I remarked, as I looked full at him,
"you've made rather a quick change, haven't you?"

"It's the running," he replied, mopping himself with
a handkerchief, and leaving his countenance like a half-
washed chess-board, "we're in for another six hours'
stew, and my phiz is plastic—I'd better be moving on,
lest I meet any of my partners; I might break some
hearts, you know; but what I wanted to say was, Don't
go making a fool of yourself, Mr. Sutton, over that little
witch with the black eyes, and don't, if you love your
life, put yourself for a moment in the power of her long-
tongued father."

This utterly surprising rejoinder was given without a
suspicion of concern or bombast. Many people would
have resented it as an impertinence, and a dishonour-
able slander upon one whose hospitality we had just
enjoyed; but I had not been a dealer in jewels for ten
years without learning to recognise instantly the "pro-
fessional" tongue; and I knew that I was talking to a
man from Scotland Yard. Yet I must confess that I
laughed inwardly at the absurdity of his fears. Few
men had come to London with stronger recommendation
than Kershaw Klein, and even the banks had trusted
him implicitly.

"Are you sure that you are making no mistake?" I
asked, as he buttoned up his coat and looked about for a
hansom. "You gentlemen have been wofully out lately;
I can't forget that one of you cautioned me against
Count Hevilick three months ago, and if I'd listened to

him I should be worth five thousand less than I am at this moment. If this man is what you think, he's managed to blind a good many big people—and his own Embassy into the bargain."

He thought for some minutes before he answered me, standing with his hands in his pockets and his cigar pointing upwards from the extreme corner of his mouth. His reply was given with a pitying smile, and was patronising—as are the replies of men convinced but unable to convince.

"Well," he said, exhaling tremendous clouds of smoke, "what I know I know; and what I don't know my wits will find out for me. I gave you the tip because you've done me—though you don't know it—a good many services; but whether you take it or leave it, that's your look out. Only, and this is my last word, don't come complaining to me if the witch walks off with your goods—and don't write to the *Times* if her father cracks your skull."

He had turned on his heel before I could utter another word; and he left me to walk slowly and thoughtfully to Bayswater, divided in my musings between the vision of the Chilian girl's beauty and the jewels of mine which she wore; but for which her father had not paid. I can only set it down to absurd infatuation; but I admit unhesitatingly that I did not very much care then whether the financial part of the business left me lacking the money or possessed of it. A rash disregard for expense is the surest sign that a woman has interested you; a longing to pay her milliner's bills is a necessary instinct to the disposition for marriage. I was at that time, and in the exhilaration of wish that came of the power of morning, quite ready to let so perfect a creature remain indebted to me for anything; and this

was natural since the spice of a little suspicion is often
the most attractive flavour in a woman's character.
But the question of the treasure of White Creek was
another matter altogether. The great diamond was not
my own, although it lay at that time in my safe in Bond
Street. It was the property of a syndicate, in which I
held a third of the shares; but the others looked to me
for the safe disposal of the stone, and for the profit of ten
thousand pounds which we hoped to get by its sale.
My responsibility, then, was no usual one; and the
barest suggestion that I was trafficking with a swindler
was enough to set me itching with anxiety.

I went home in this mood, but not to sleep. A fever-
ish dreaming—chiefly of a seductive girl with black-
brown wavy hair and black eyes that searched and
fascinated with an inexplicable spell—served me for
rest; and at eleven o'clock I was at my office, and the
Chilian was with me. He was a man of fine presence,
a long black beard falling upon his ample chest, and a
certain refinement of carriage and bearing giving him
a dignity which is not usual in an American. The
object of his visit was twofold, to pay the bill he owed
me, and to tell me that his partner, Hermann Rudisic,
would reach London from Valparaiso in a week's time;
when he would bring him to me to complete the purchase of the great stone. He said further that as the
season was over he had taken a place near Basingstoke,
the Woodfields it was named; and that he hoped his
daughter, who did not do well in an English climate,
would benefit by the wealth of pine-trees about the
house. He finished by giving me a reference to his
London bankers, and also another to one of the best
known of the financiers in Lombard Street. In due
course I communicated with both firms, and received

answers which set every doubt about the financial position of Kershaw Klein at rest. The bankers declared
that I might trust him unhesitatingly for such a sum as
I named. The other replied that the Colonel's brother
was of great standing and position in Chili, and that he
himself carried letters which proved his undoubted
probity. More complete vindication could not be had;
and I went home to laugh consumedly at the gentleman
who had found such a mare's nest, and to wonder if my
friends would laugh very much if they heard—how little
I thought at that time of the old pleasantries with which
I had once greeted the tidings of a marriage.

I did not hear more of Klein for some fifteen days,
at the end of which time he wrote saying that Hermann
Rudisic was with him at Basingstoke; and that they
hoped to call upon me on the following Friday. The
march of events was from that time quick. On the
Thursday I read in a daily paper of an accident in
Berkshire to a Chilian visitor, who had been thrown
from his carriage and seriously hurt. The account said
that his life was despaired of, and that he was then
lying at the house of his host, the well-known Colonel
Kershaw Klein, who had taken Lord Aberly's place, the
Woodfields. On the Friday morning I received a long
letter from the Colonel deploring the accident and the
delay, more especially because his commission to purchase the stone extended only to the 10th of August, and
it was then the third. He hoped, however, that matters
would look brighter at the end of that time; and would
bring his partner to London the moment he could travel.

Now, at the first thought, this intelligence set all
the inherent suspicion, which is a part of me, at work
once more. Suggestions of doubt rose again and again,
instantly to be suppressed. Had I not satisfied myself

completely as to the Colonel's standing, his means, his reputation, and his personal character? Was he not staying in Lord Aberly's house? Had not he passed most brilliantly through a London season? Were there not twenty members of the Bachelors' Club seeking to pay for the sake of his daughter the fine imposed upon amorous backsliders? If one were to suspect every man with such credentials as these, the sooner one shut one's door, and locked one's safe for good, the better for all hope of doing business. Of all this I was certain; and had already come to the determination to put from my mind suspicion both of the Count and his daughter, when there came to me by the afternoon delivery another letter concerning the matter; but this was anonymous, and in a hand I did not know. It was a curious scrawl written upon a slip of account paper, and its contents were but these words:—

"You will be asked to Kershaw Klein's house in three days. I told you the other morning not to trust yourself with the man; I say now, accept the invitation."

This was plainly from my friend of Hyde Park; and I confess that his pompous mysteriousness and pretence of knowledge amused me. Even he no longer complained of Colonel Klein's reputation, nor advised me now to avoid him. His letter finally quieted my scruples, and from that moment I resolved to dally with them no longer; and to let no silly fears delay the negotiations for the sale of the treasure of White Creek.

In this resolution I waited rather anxiously for the coming of Klein and his partner, but three days went, and I saw nothing of them; it being on the Monday morning at eleven o'clock that the former drove up to Bond Street in a single brougham, and came with his daughter into my private office. He seemed in a great state of distress, saying that Rudisic, although better, was still unable to set foot to the ground; and begging me as the time was so short to take the great jewel to Berkshire—his house was just across the line dividing the county from Hampshire—and there to settle the matter that very day. I heard him mechanically; my eyes glued on the exquisite picture which his daughter made; her gown of white delaine showing the mature contour of her figure admirably; and her deep brown hair rolling from the shelter of a great straw hat in silken waves upon her shoulders. If she had fascinated me at the dance, the fascination was intensified there. I would cheerfully have risked the best parcel of rubies in the place to have had the pleasure of keeping her in the office even for an hour; and I did not hesitate one moment in accepting Klein's offer.

"Come down to-day," said he, "and bring your man with you in case we don't do business, and you have to return alone. I don't like mailing with big stuff on me; you never know who gets wind of it. I suppose you have somebody you could take."

Even with the girl's eyes upon me and her laughing threat to "make me tramp at tennis awhile," I had a measure of satisfaction in this request, and thought instantly of Abel.

"Yes," said I with a light laugh, "I will bring my own detective. He's down below now."

"That's right," said Klein, "and we'll catch the two-forty from Waterloo. I've ordered the carriage to meet that, and there's just time for a snack between whiles. Never forget your food, sir—I don't for all the business in Europe. I once lost a commission for a railway in Venezuela through a sandwich—but there that's another story, and I'll tell it you over a chop at the Criterion. I guess I've got an appetite on, and so's Margaret, eh, little girl?"

He slapped his chest to signify that a void was there; and we all went off down Piccadilly, returning afterwards for the gem which I had placed in a flat-velvet case. I put it into my jewel pocket, cunningly contrived in my vest, and with no more delay we got to Waterloo and to our saloon, Abel travelling second class, by the bye, and in another compartment. There was a well-

THE FOOTMAN.

turned-out waggonette to meet us when we reached Basingstoke; and after a drive of something under an hour through some of that glorious pine scenery of southern Berkshire, we entered a short drive edged by thick laurels, and were shortly at the gate of the Woodfields. Of the exterior of the house I saw nothing, for, as I descended from the waggonette, I chanced to catch the eye of the footman, who had a finger to his lips; and an exclamation almost broke from my lips. Notwithstanding his disguise I recognised the man in a moment. He was the "Oxford youth" who had given me a cigar in the park on the morning after the dance in Grosvenor Crescent.

The discovery was not a pleasant one. It made discord of all the music of Margaret Klein's voice—she was quickly babbling to me in the old Georgian Hall—and forbade my taking considerable notice of the massive oak of the double staircase, or of the exceedingly bright-nosed "ancestors" who smiled upon us from twenty gilt frames. Abel had come up to my room with me, I pretending that he invariably acted as my valet; and once inside a very large but very ugly square bedchamber, whose windows overlooked the prim lawn and terrace of flowers, I shut the door and had a word with him.

"Abel," said I, "that footman who drove us from the station must be one of the Scotland Yard lot; what's he doing in this house?"

Abel whistled, and by instinct I suppose put his hand upon his pistol pocket.

"Have you got your revolver with you, sir?" he asked.

"Of course I have; and I'll take this opportunity to charge all the chambers, but I don't believe for a moment there will be occasion to use it. The man's on a false scent entirely. It's necessary at the same time to act like wise men, and not like fools; and I must count on you to be near me while we're in the place. If there's any knavery afoot, we sha'nt hear of it until the place is asleep; but come here when I am going to bed, and then we shall know what to do."

I sent him off with this to the servants' quarters, and dressed, though an indescribable sense of nervousness had taken hold of me; and I found myself peering into every

cupboard and cranny like an old woman looking for a
burglar. The situation was either as dangerous as it
could be, or I was the victim of farcical fears. Yet the
very shadows across the immense floor, and the aureola
upon the carpet about the dressing table seemed to give
gloom to the chamber. So thick were the walls of the
old house that no sound reached me from the rooms
below; and when the gong struck the hour for dinner
its note reverberated as a wave of deadened sound
through some curtained chapel or chill vault. What did
it mean, I kept asking myself; the illness, was it sham?
the man from London, was he on a fool's errand? my
visit, was it foolhardy? Had I walked into a trap
at the bidding of a pretty woman? Were all the guarantees I had received in the Colonel's favour fraudulent or
mistaken? I could not think so. Again and again I
told myself that the fellow from Scotland Yard was an
absurd crank upon a false scent, and that ninety
jewellers of a hundred would have done as I had done,
and have brought the stone to Berkshire. And with this
thought I took a better courage and hastily finished my
dressing. I need scarce say that I had the jewel in my
pocket when I went to the drawing-room, and that I had
already determined that it should not leave me for a
moment. I got rid, however, of more of my fears when
I entered the artistic and homely room where Margaret
Klein was waiting; and in the brighter scene of light
and laughter the absurdity of suspicion again occurred
to me.

The meal was an excellent one, admirably served;
the wine was perfect. I sat at my host's right facing his
daughter, who seemed to exert herself unusually to
fascinate, making delicate play with her speaking eyes;
and promising me all the possibilities of Berkshire rest,

if I cared to stay with them over the week. To this her father, the Colonel, who had the ribbon of an Order in his buttonhole, and looked exceedingly handsome, added,—

"And I hope you will, for you're not seeming as well as you were last week. You people in England live in too narrow a circle. A voyage across the pond makes an epoch in your lives; you are scarce prepared to admit yet that there is any other city but London. If you would enlarge the scope of your actions, you would grumble less—and perhaps, if I may say so, allow that other nations share some of your best boasted qualities. Now I am truly cosmopolitan; I regard no city as my home; I would as soon set out on a voyage of three thousand miles as of five. I come to England, and I do it in ten days from Land's End to John o' Groat's; and when I think I'll rest awhile I ask, Where is your pretty county? and I settle for three weeks to explore it."

"I hope Mr. Sutton will do the same," said Margaret, following up his invitation. "I want to learn all about the dames who won't know you unless you had a grandfather; and I should like to see a curate who is passing rich on forty pounds a year. I guess we mean to go right in now we're amongst your best folk."

"I'll stay a day or two with pleasure if you will pilot me," said I, as she rose to go to the drawing-room; but I little knew that my visit was to terminate abruptly in three hours or less, or what was to happen in the between-time.

A lean, lank-looking butler served the Colonel and myself with coffee when she had gone; and after that my host took me to the drawing-room, where I found her engaged in the pursuit of trying over a "coster" song. The Colonel suggested business at once, saying,—

"I'll leave you with Margaret while I go up to Hermann and learn if he's well enough to receive us; I dare say you can amuse yourselves. I sha'nt be gone five minutes."

He was really away for twenty minutes; but I did not count the time. The whole situation seemed so curious—on the one hand a London detective playing footman in the house, on the other a delightful host, and a girl whose every word fascinated and whose every motion drew you instinctively to her—that I gave up any attempt to solve it; and beyond the knowledge that I had reason to be watchful, I put no restraint upon myself; but sat at her side while she played the lightest of music; or occasionally lent back to speak to me, so that her hair brushed my face and her eyes almost looked into mine.

"It was good of you to come," she almost whispered in one of these pauses, glancing up timorously, and speaking altogether in the sympathetic tone.

"Do you miss the excitement of London?" I asked, letting my hand rest for a moment on hers.

"I guess not," she replied; "but I miss some one who can talk to me as you talk; you're going to stop awhile, aren't you?"

"I'll stop as long as you ask me to."

When he was gone she went on playing for some minutes, turning away at last impatiently from the piano, and facing round with a serious, almost alarmed look. What she meant to say or do I cannot tell, for at that moment the Colonel came back and told us that his partner was in the dressing-room upstairs, and would be glad to see me at once.

H

"Margaret may come too?" he asked me. "She would like to see the great stone."

"Of course," I replied; "it will be a pleasure to show it to her."

I cannot tell you why it was, but as we rose together to leave the room I seemed in a moment to realize that the affair had come to a crisis. In that instant, notwithstanding guarantees, references, Margaret Klein's fascinations, and the hundred arguments I had so often used to convince myself of the folly of suspicion, there came to me as distinct and clear a warning as though some human voice had given speech to it. The very silence of the others—for they said no word, and a curious hesitation seemed to come upon them—impressed the conviction of the monition. Once in the hall, my uneasiness became stronger, for there at a table was the footman I had recognised, and as he glanced at me when I passed him his face was knit up as the face of a man thinking; and he let a glass fall at the very moment we reached the stairs. What he wished to convey I do not know; but although I felt there was danger in leaving the ground floor, another force dragged me on behind the Colonel, and kept me advancing unhesitatingly until I had reached the end of the long picture-gallery with him, and he had knocked upon a door in the eastern wing of the rambling mansion. What this force was I do not pretend to explain. It may have been merely the influence of the woman; it may have been my inherent obstinacy and belief in myself; or simple lack of conviction which forbade any public expression of the fears I had fomented. I know only that we waited for some seconds in the passage until a hospital nurse opened the door, and that I found myself at last in a very pretty boudoir, where a pale and sickly-looking man was lying upon a couch, but propped up to greet us. The formalities of introduction were accomplished by the Colonel with great suavity and grace; and the nurse having set chairs at the side of the sick man's couch, and placed a table there, she withdrew, and we were ready for the business.

"A PALE AND SICKLY-LOOKING MAN WAS LYING UPON A COUCH."

That you should understand what happened in the next few minutes it is necessary for me to say a word upon the construction of the boudoir. It was a room hung in pink silk and white, and it had two doors in it, giving off to other rooms, whose size I could not see since they were in darkness. For light, we had a lamp with a white shade upon the invalid's table, and two others upon the mantel-shelf; while we were seated in a fashion that allayed any fears I might have had of personal and sudden attack. The Colonel lounged in an American rocking-chair, he being nearest to the head of the couch; his daughter leant back against a buhl-work cabinet, she being a little way from the sick man's feet; I had a library-chair, and was alone in an attitude which would allow me to spring to my defence —if that were necessary—without delay. I looked, too, at Hermann Rudisic, the Colonel's partner, and I confess that contempt for his physical powers was my first thought. I was convinced that if it were a question of fight, I could hold the two men until Abel, who was in the servants' hall, came to my assistance; and while the others were present I had no fear of any of those wild machinations which are chiefly the property of imaginative fiction-makers. This knowledge gave to me my nerve again, and without more ado I took the case from my pocket and showed the stone.

The vision of the glorious gem, rippling on its surface with a myriad lights, white, and golden, and many-coloured, in the play of radiating fire, was one that compelled the silence of amazed admiration for many minutes. Margaret Klein first spoke, her face bent to the diamond so that its waves of colour seemed to float up to her ravished eyes; and with a little cry wrung from her satisfaction she said,—

"Oh, Mr. Sutton, it's too beautiful to look at!"

"I am glad that it does not disappoint," said I.

"It could disappoint no one," the invalid said, stretch-

ing out a hand which trembled to draw the treasure
closer to his eyes.

"It's the whitest stone I've seen for three years," the
Colonel remarked coolly, and then, as with a new
thought, he added,—

"I believe it's whiter than the Brazilian stone in my
old ring. I should like to compare them, if you'll let
me? The other stuff is in my dressing-room there;
Margaret, will you get it?"

He gave her his keys, and taking a lamp from the
shelf, she passed into the chamber which was behind
me. In the same moment Rudisic asked his host to prop
him up higher upon the couch, and the Colonel had just
begun to place the pillows when I heard Margaret's
voice crying,—

"Father, I can't open the drawer—it's stuck; do come
and help."

It was an act of consummate folly—that I concede
you; but I was so completely unaware of any signs
of trickery here, and had so forgotten my fears, that I
found it the most natural thing in the world to step into
the room, and to enjoy helping the girl in her difficulty.
I discovered her before an open door—the door of a
wardrobe I thought it was for a moment, but I saw at
the second look that it gave access to a tiny chamber,
whereof the walls were all drawers. Margaret Klein
herself stood within this curiously fashioned safe, built
as part of the house, and was still struggling with the
refractory drawer; so that I had no hesitation—nor,
indeed, thought suspiciously—in going to her side. She
laughed slyly as we stood in the semi-dark together,
and my hand falling by chance on hers, she pressed it,
and put her face very close to mine—so close, that to
have resisted kissing her would have been a crime for

which a man would have repented until his last day.
I cannot tell accurately how long I held her in a passionate embrace, feeling her lips glued upon my own;
but suddenly and quickly she pushed me from her with
a surprising strength of arm, and before I could regain
my balance she had sprung into the room, and the door
of the small chamber in which I was left swung to with
a clang, striking me backwards as it pressed upon me,
and coming nigh to stunning me. So thick was this
door, so impenetrable, that its closing was succeeded
by the stillness of vault or catacomb. I had scarce
realized the whole trick, or the terrible predicament
sheer folly had placed me in, when I was plunged into
the abyss of utter darkness, shut as it were into the
coffin that had been prepared for me. A frightful panic,
a hideous terror, an indescribable anger, came upon me
from the very first moment of that fearful trial. For
some minutes—the first minutes of imprisonment in a
room where I could stand my height with difficulty, but
whose iron sides my elbows touched as I turned—I
think my reason must have been paralysed. Rage,
shame of my folly, yet, above all, unsurpassable fear,
drove me to beat with my fists upon the door, which
gave me back the touch of solid steel; to cry out aloud
as a man in the throes of painful death; to grind my
teeth until pain shot into my brain; to forget, in fact,
that I was from that time helpless, and that others alone
could give to me life.

When the first great terror had passed, and a mental
struggle had left me with some sense, I leant against
the steel door, and thought again of my fate. I had
little science, yet I knew that the hours of any man,
shut in an air-tight chamber such as that room of steel
was, could be few. I had heard that asphyxiation was

"I CANNOT TELL ACCURATELY HOW LONG I HELD HER IN A PASSIONATE EMBRACE."

a peaceful death, and think I could have had courage
to face if a little light had been given to me. But I was
in utter weighty darkness; I could not even see that
dull red light as of one's own soul shining, which may
come in the gentler dark of night. There was only
upon me that sense of impenetrable blackness, the grim
feeling that I had come to my coffin, had slept in it, and
arisen to this unspeakable terror. My whole being then
seemed to cry aloud for sight, one moment in which
living light should again shine upon me. A great craving for air; a sense of terrible effort in the lungs, a
rushing of blood to the head—these things succeeded,
and as I suffered them flashes of thought came and
passed, hope extended a hand to me, processes of reasoning told me that I should be saved, only to convince me
the more that I should die.

If I could have reasoned sanely I should have seen
that my hope was all bound up in Abel and the detective in the house. Klein, and the invalid, and the girl—
they had been gone long since, unless others had put
hands upon them. My own servant, I knew, would seek
for me first; but even if he came to the safe, how would
he open it, how cut through these inches of steel before
death had ended it all? It was even possible that the
door of the strong room was a concealed door—and so
afterwards I proved it to be. In that case, how would
they know even of my necessity? These torturing re-
flections threw at last a glimmer of necessary activity
upon my despair. I raised my voice, though I had then
the strangest sensation in my veins, and my heart was
pumping audibly ; and for many minutes I shouted with
all my strength. Once I thought that I heard, even
through the door, some sound from the other room; yet
when I cried louder, and beat again upon the steel, there

"I FIRED THREE ROUNDS FROM THE REVOLVER INTO THE ROOM."

was no signal. I remained unheeded; my voice gradually failed me; I could cry no longer, but began to sink almost into a coma.

How long this coma lasted I cannot tell. I was roused from it, after a hideous dream of waiting, by sounds of knocking upon some wall near me; and with a new strength I shouted again, and beat again upon the door of steel. Yet, I knew that I was not heard for the sound of the blows grew fainter and were passing away and—life, which had come near again, seemed to pass with them. Then was my supreme moment of misery, yet one giving an inspiration which brought me here to write this record. Recoiling from the door as the knocks without grew fainter, I struck my back against the iron wall, and my pistol, which I had forgotten, pressed into my flesh. Regardless of all thought of consequences, of the path of the bullet, or the effect upon me of the stifling smoke, I fired three rounds from the revolver into the room—and instantly was breathing the densest smoke. Then a sudden faintness took me; and I recollect only that I fell forward into a world of light, and there slept.

*   ⚬   ❊   ⚬   ⚬   ❊

"The joke was, seeing you living, Mr. Sutton, that Abel swallowed the wine that butler gave him, and was made as insensibly drunk as a man who takes stage chloroform. I knew all along that the butler was the one to watch; and while I never thought they'd do you mischief in the room—believing they meant to work after midnight—my men in the grounds clapped the bracelets on the lank chap up by the woods there, and he had the diamond on him."

"And the Colonel and his daughter and the invalid?"

I asked, raising myself in the bed of an upper chamber
of the Woodfields, on the foot of which sat my old friend
the detective of Hyde Park.

"Got clear away by a back staircase we'd never
heard of, through a cellar and a passage to the lower
grounds! They knocked old Jimmy, the local policeman, on the head by the spinney, and all they left him
was a bump as big as an orange. That girl must have
had a liking for you. One of my men nearly took her
as she jumped into a dog-cart; but she threw the keys
in his face, and he brought them here. I knew nothing
about this room, and shouldn't have done except for the
ring of your revolver; but the last Lord Aberly built it
to take his famous collection of rubies and emeralds, and
that lag Klein evidently heard of it, and leased the place
furnished on that account."

"How do you know that he was a swindler?"

"I heard of him in New York when I was there last
winter. He was wanted for the great mail robbery near
St. Louis. A clever scoundrel, too; deceived a heap of
folk by forged letters of introduction, and the banks by
leaving big deposits with them. He must be worth a
pretty pile; but I don't doubt he came over here from
America on purpose to steal your diamonds. He was
out at the Cape nine months ago, and got to hear all
about the White Creek stone. Then he must have
known that Herbert Klein, his supposed brother, and a
real rich man of Valparaiso, was away yachting in the
Pacific; and so he claimed him, and traded on his undoubted couple of million. A clever forger, and the
other two with him nearly as smart. It was lucky for
you that one of the grooms here had heard of a mysterious place in that dressing-room, and led me, when I
missed you, to tap the walls. You were nearly done

for, and though you don't know, you've been in bed pretty well a week."

"And the man's daughter ?" I asked, a little anxiously.

"His daughter," he replied; "pshaw, she's his wife! —and we'll take the pair of them yet."

But he never did, although the lank butler is now our guest at Dartmoor.

THE ACCURSED GEMS

THE ACCURSED GEMS

THE accursed gems lie sedately in the lowest drawer of my strong room, shining from a couple of dozen of prim leather cases, with a light which is full of strange memories. I call them accursed because I can not sell them; yet there are those with other histories, stones about which the fancy of romance has sported, and the strong hand of tragedy has touched with an indelible brand. It may be that the impulse of sentiment, working deep down in the heart of the ostensibly commercial character, forbids me to cry some of these wares in the market-place with any vigour; it may be that the play of chance moves the mind of the jewel-buyer to a prejudice against them. In any case, they lie in my safe unhonoured and unsung—and, lacking that which Sewell called the "precious balsam" of reputation, are merely so much carbon or mineral matter giving light to iron walls which give no light again.

For the stones which have no history I am not an apologist. Some day, those excellent people who now decry them in every salon where jewels are discussed, will give up the hope of attempting to buy them cheaply; and I shall make my profit. Everything comes to him who *can* wait, and I am not in a hurry. As to the others, which have been the pivots of romance or serious story, they may well lie as they are while they serve my memory in the jotting down of some of these mysteries.

And that they do serve it I have no measure of doubt. Here, for instance, is a little bag of pearls and diamonds. It contains a black pearl from Koepang, so rich in silvery lustre, and so perfect in shape, that it should be worth eight hundred pounds in any market in Europe; a couple of pink pearls from the Bahamas, of fine orient yet pear-shaped, and therefore less valuable as fashion dictates; five old Brazilian diamonds averaging two carats each; a number of smaller diamonds for finish; and two great white pearls, which I find at the very bottom of the bag. Those stones were bought by the late Lord Maclaren a month before the date announced for his marriage with the Hon. Christine King. He had intended them as his gift to her, a handsome and sufficient gift, it must be admitted, yet so did fickle fortune work that his very generosity was the indirect cause of a commotion in the week of the wedding, and of as pretty a social scandal as society has known for a decade.

The matter was hushed up of course. For six weeks, as a wag said, it was a nine days' wonder. Aged ladies discussed it from every point of view, but could make nothing of it. The Society papers lacked enough information to lie about it. The principal actors held their tongues, and in due time the West forgot, for a new scandal arose, and the courts supplied the craving for the doubtful, which is a part of polite education nowadays. Yet I do not think that I make a boastful claim, in asserting that I alone, beyond those immediately concerned, became possessed of full knowledge of the occurrence. It was to me first of all that Lord Maclaren related the history of it, and, despite my advice to the contrary, laid it upon me that I should tell none in his lifetime. He is dead now, and the publication of the story will throw a light upon much

that is well worth investigating. It may also help me
to sell the pearls, which is infinitely more important, as
any unprejudiced person will admit.

Here then is the story. I had a visit from the chief
actor in it towards the end of June in the year 1890.
He came to tell me that he was to be married quietly in
the middle of the following month to the Hon. Christine
King, the very beautiful sister of Lord Cantiliffe. She
was then staying at the old family place at St. Peters,

LORD MACLAREN.

in Kent; and she wished to avoid a public wedding in
view of the recent death of her sister, whose beauty was
no less remarkable than her own. Maclaren's visit was
but the prelude to the purchase of a present, and the
business was made the easier since he had the simplest
notions as to his requirements. He had recently come
from America—without a wife *mirabile dictu*—and there
had seen a curious anchor bracelet. The wristband of
this bauble was formed of a plain gold cable, the anchor

I

itself of pearls and diamonds; the shackle consisted of a small circle of brilliants; the shaft had a pink pearl at either end; the shank had a black pearl at the foot of it, and the flukes were of white pearls with small diamonds round them. I found it to be rather a vulgar ornament; but his heart was set on having it, and it chanced that I had the very pearls necessary. I told him that I would make him a model, and send it down to his hotel at Ramsgate within a week; and that, if he then thought the jewel to be over showy, we could refashion it. He left much pleased, returning by the Granville express to Kent; and within the week he had the model; and I received his instructions to proceed with the work.

It is necessary, I think, to say a word here about this curious character. At the time I knew him, Maclaren was a man in his fortieth year, though he looked older. He was once vulgarly described in a club smoking-room as being "all hair and teeth," like a buzzard; and his best friend could not have ranked him with the handsome. Yet the women liked him—perhaps because it was a tradition that he made love to every pretty girl in town; and it was surprising beyond belief that he reached his fortieth year, and remained single. When he went to America in 1888 the whole of the prophets gave him six months of celibacy; but he cheated them, and returned without a wife. True, a copy of an American society paper was passed round the club, where the men learnt with surprise that New York had believed this elderly Don Juan to be engaged to Evelyn Lenox, "the lady of the unlimited dollars," as young Barisbroke of the Bachelors' called her; and had been very indignant when he took passage by the *Teutonic*, and left her people to face the titters of a triumphant rivalry. But

for all that he was not married, and could afford to
laugh at the malignant scribes who made couplets of
his supposed amatory adventures in Boston; and dedi-
cated sonnets of apology, "*pro amore mea*," to E——
L—— and the marrying mothers of New York generally. Such a man cared little for the threats of this
young lady's brother, or for the common rumour that
she was the most dashing girl in New York city, and
would make things unpleasant for him. He had twenty
thousand a year, and for *fiancée* one of the prettiest
roses in the whole garden of Kent. What harm then
could a broker's daughter, three thousand miles away,
do to him? or how mar his happiness?

But I am anticipating, and must hark back to the
anchor with the flukes of pearl. I sent the model down
on Wednesday; on the Friday morning I received the
order to proceed with the work. Early on the following
Monday, as I read my paper in a cab on the way to
Bond Street, I saw a tremendous headline which announced the "sudden and mysterious disappearance of
Lord Maclaren." The report said that he had left his
hotel on the Saturday afternoon to walk, as the supposition went, to St. Peters. But he had never reached
Lord Cantiliffe's house; and although search had been
made by the police and by special coastguard parties,
no trace of him had been found. I need scarcely say
that the murder theory was set up at once. Clever men
from town came down to wag their heads with stupid
men from Canterbury, and to discuss the "only possible
theory," of which there were a dozen or more. The
police arrested all the drunken men within a radius of
ten miles, and looked for bloodstains on their coats.
The Hon. Christine King was spoken of as "distracted,"
which was possible; and the family of the missing

nobleman as "plunged into the most profound grief."
Nor, as an eloquent special reporter in his best mood
explained, was this supposed tragedy made less painful
by the knowledge that the unhappy victim of accident
or of murder was to have been married within the'
month.

For a whole week the press had no other topic; the
police telegraphed to all the capitals; a reward of a
thousand pounds was offered for knowledge of Lord
Maclaren, " last seen upon the East Cliff at Ramsgate at
three o'clock on the afternoon of Saturday, the fifth of
July." A hundred tongues gave you the exact details
of an imagined assassination; ten times that number—
and these tongues chiefly feminine—told you that he
had shirked the marriage upon its very threshold. But
the mystery remained unexplained—and as the day for
the wedding drew near, the excitement amongst a sec-
tion of society rose to fever heat. Had the body been
found? Had the detectives a clue? Were the strange
hints—implying that the missing man had quarrelled
with his *fiancée's* brother, and thrown a glass of wine in
his face; that he had a wife in Algiers; that he was
married a year ago at Cyprus; that he was bankrupt—
merely the fable of malicious tongues, or had they that
germ of truth from which so vast a disease of scandal
can grow? I made no pretence to answer the questions
—but they interested me, and I watched for the development of the story with the keenness of a hardened
novel reader.

The day fixed for the wedding now drew near; and
when the bridegroom did not appear, the vulgar, who
do not believe scandals though they like to hear them,
declared that the murder theory was true beyond question. The rest said that he was either bankrupt or

bigamist—and having consoled themselves with the reflection, they let the matter go. It is likely that I should have done the same had I not enjoyed a solution of the mystery, which came to me unsought and accidentally. On a day near to that fixed for the wedding I was at Victoria Station about eight o'clock in the evening when I ran full upon the missing noble-man; and for some while stood speechless with as-tonishment at the sight of him. His beard was longer than ever, recalling the traditions of Killingworthe or of Johann Mayo; his Dundreary whiskers were shaggy and unkempt; he was very pale in the face, and wore a little yachting cap and a blue serge suit which be-garbed him ridiculously. He had no luggage with him, not even a valise; and his first remark was given in the voice of a man afraid, and in a measure broken.

"Ah, Sutton, that's you, is it?" he cried. "I'm glad to see you, by Jove; have you such a thing as half-a-crown in your pocket?"

I offered him half-a-sovereign, still saying nothing; but he continued rapidly,—

"You've heard all about it, of course—what are they saying here now? Do they think I'm a dead man, eh?—but I won't face them yet. Upon my life, I dare not see a soul. Come with me to an hotel; there's a good fellow—but let's have a cognac first; I'm shivering like a child with a fever."

I gave him some brandy at a bar, and after that we took a four wheeled cab—he insisting on the privacy—and drove to a private hotel in Cecil-street, Strand. They did not know him there, and I engaged a room for him and ordered dinner, taking these things upon myself, since he was as helpless as a babe. After the meal he seemed somewhat better, and I telegraphed to

Ramsgate for his man, though it was impossible that the fellow could be with him until the following morning. In the meantime I found myself doing valet's work for him—but I had his story; and although it was not until some months later that another supplied some of the missing links in it, he telling me the barest outline, I will set it down here plainly as a narrative, and without any of those "says I's" and "says he's," which were the particular abomination of Defoe, as they have been of many since his day.

The complete explanation of this mystery was one, I think, to astonish most people. It was so utterly unlooked for, that I was led at the first hearing to believe the narrator insane. He told me that at three o'clock on the afternoon of July 5th, he had left his hotel on the East Cliff at Ramsgate—the day being glorious, and a full sun playing upon the Channel and many ships— and had determined to walk over to St. Peters, where his *fiancée* expected him to a tennis party. With this intention, he struck along the cliff towards Broadstairs, but had gone only a few paces, when a seaman stopped him, and touching his hat respectfully, said that he had a message for him.

"Well, my man, what is it?" Maclaren asked—I had the dialogue from the seaman himself—being in a hurry as those who walk the ways of love usually are.

"My respects to your honour," replied the fellow, "but the ketch *Bowery*, moored off the pier-head, 'ud be glad to see your honour if convenient, and if not, maybe to-morrow?"

"What the devil does the man mean?" cried his lordship, but the seaman plucking up courage continued,—

"An old friend of your honour's for sure he is, my

guv'ner, Abraham Burrow, what you had the acquant-
ance of in New York city."

"'WELL, MY MAN, WHAT IS IT?' MACLAREN ASKED."

"Well, and why can't he come ashore? I remember
the man perfectly—I have every cause to"—a true

remark since Abraham Burrow then owed the speaker some two thousand pounds; and had shown no unprincipled desire to pay it.

"The fact is, my lordship," replied the seaman, whose vocabulary was American and strange, "the fact is he's tidy sick, on his beam ends, I guess with brounchitis; and he won't be detaining you not as long as a bosun's whistle if you'll go aboard, and be easin' of him."

Now, although this comparatively juvenile lover was in a mighty hurry to get to St. Peters, there was yet a powerful financial motive to send him to the ship. He had done business with this Abraham Burrow in America; the man had—we won't say swindled—but been smart enough there to relieve him of a couple of thousand pounds. To hope for the recovery of such a sum seemed as childish as a sigh for the moon. Maclaren had not seen Burrow for twelve months, and did not know a moment before this meeting whether he was alive or dead. Yet here he was in a yacht off Ramsgate harbour, desiring to see his creditor, and to see him immediately. The latter reflected that such a visit would not occupy half an hour of his time, that it may lead to the recovery of some part of his money, that he could make his excuses to the pretty girl awaiting him —in short, he went with the seaman; and in a quarter of an hour he stepped on board an exceedingly well-kept yacht, which lay beyond the buoy over against the East Pier; and all his trouble began.

The craft, as I have said, was ketch rigged, and must have been of seventy tons or more. There was a good square saloon aft, and a couple of tiny cabins, the one amidships, the other at the poop. When Lord Maclaren went aboard, three seamen and a boy were the occu-

pants of the deck; but a King Charles spaniel barked at
the top of the companion; and a steward came presently
and asked the visitor to go below. He descended to the
saloon at this; but the sick man, they told him, lay in
the fore cabin; and thither he followed his very obse-
quious guide.

I had the account of this episode and of much that
follows from two sources, one a man I met in New
York last summer, the other, the victim of the singularly American conspiracy. Lord Maclaren's account
was simple—"As there's a heaven above me, Sutton,"
said he, "I'd no sooner put my foot in the hole when
the door was slammed behind me, and bolted like a
prison gate." The American said, "I guess the old boy
had hardly walked right in, before they'd hitched up
the latch, and he was shouting glory. Then the
skipper let the foresail go—for the ketch was only
lying-to, and in ten minutes he was standing out down
Channel. But you never heard such a noise as there
was below in all your days. Talk about a sheet and
pillow-case party in an insane asylum, that's no word
for it."

The fact that the "illustrious nobleman," as the
penny society papers called him, was trapped admitted
of no question. He realized it himself in a few moments, and sat down to wonder, "who and why the
devil, etc.," in five languages. I need scarcely say that
the thing was an utter and inexplicable mystery to him.
He thought at first that robbery was the motive, for he
had the model of the bracelet upon him; and as he sat
alone in the cabin, he really feared personal violence.
He told me that he waited to see the door open and a
villain enter, armed with Colt or knuckleduster, after
the traditional Adelphian mood; but a couple of hours

passed and no one came, and after that the only interruption to his meditation was the steward's knock upon
the cabin door, and his polite desire to know "Will my
lord take tea?" "My lord" told him to carry his tea to
a latitude where high temperatures prevail; and after
that, continued to kick lustily at the door, and to make
original observations upon the owner of the yacht, and
upon her crew, until the light failed. Yet no one
heeded him; and when it was dark the roll of the
yacht to the seas made him sure that they stood well
out, and were beating with a stiff-breeze.

Unto this point, temper had dominated him; but now
a quiet yet very deep alarm took its place. He began to
ask himself more seriously if his position were not one
of great danger, if he had not to face some mysterious
but very daring enemy—even if he were like to come out
of the adventure with his life. Yet his mind could not
bring to his recollection any deed that had merited vindictive anger on the part of another; nor was he a
blamable man as the world goes. He paid his debts—
every three years; he was amongst the governors of
five fashionable charities, and the only scandalous case
which concerned him was arranged between the lawyers
on the eve of its coming into court. The matrons told
you that he was "a dear delightful rogue"; the men
said that he was "a cunning old dog"; and between
them agreed that he had read the commandments at
least. Possibly, however, those hours of solitude in the
cabin compelled him to think rather of his vices than of
his virtues—and it may be that the fear was so much the
more real as his shortcomings were secret. Be that as
it may, he assured me that he had never suffered so
much as he did during that strange imprisonment, and
that he cried almost with delight when the door of the

" 'I'D NO SOONER PUT MY FOOT IN THE HOLE WHEN THE DOOR WAS
SLAMMED BEHIND ME.' "

cabin opened, and he saw the table of the saloon set for dinner, and light falling upon it from a handsome lamp below the skylight. During one delicious moment he thought himself the victim of a well-meaning practical joker—the next his limbs were limp as cloth, and he sank upon a cushioned seat with a groan which must have been heard by the men above.

This scene has been so faithfully described to me that I can see it as clearly as though I myself stood amongst the players. On the one hand, a pretty little American girl, with hands clasped and malicious laughter about her rosy mouth; on the other, a shrinking, craven, abject shadow of a man, cowering upon the cushions of a sofa, in blank astonishment, and hiding his view of her with bony fingers. At a glance you would have said that the girl was not twenty—but she was twenty-three, the picture of youth, with the colour of the sea-health upon her cheeks, the spray of the sea-foam glistening in her rich brown hair. She had upon her head a little hat of straw posed daintily; her dress was of white serge with a scarf of yacht-club colours at the throat; but her feet were the tiniest in the world, and the brown shoes which hid them not unfit for an artist's model. And as she stood laughing at the man who had become her guest upon the yacht, her attitude would have made the fortune of half the painters in Hampstead. The two faced each other thus silently for a few minutes, but she was the first to speak, her voice overflowing with rippling laughter.

"Well," she said, "I call this real good of you, my lord, to come on my yacht—when you were just off to the other girl—and your wedding's fixed for the eighteenth of July. My word, you're the kindest-hearted man in Europe."

He looked up at her, some shame marked in his eyes, and he said,—

"Evelyn, I—I—never thought it was you!"

"Then how pleased you must be. Oh, I'm right glad, I tell you; I'm just as pleased as you are. To think that we've never met since you left N'York in such a flurry that you hadn't time even to send me a line—but of course you men are so busy and so smart that girls' don't count, and I knew you were just dying to see me, and I sent the boat off saying it was old Burrow—how you love Burrow!—and here you are, my word!"

She spoke labouring under a heavy excitement, so that her sentences flowed over one another. But he could scarce find a coherent word, and began to tremble as she went on,—

"You'll stay awhile, of course, and—why, you're as pale as spectres, I guess. Now if you look like that I shall begin to think that we're not the old friends we were in N'York a year ago, and walk right upstairs to Arthur. You remember my brother Arthur, of course you do. He was your particular friend, wasn't he?—but how you boys quarrel. They really told me two months ago in the city that Arthur was going in the shooting business with you. Fancy that now, and at your age."

This sentence revealed what was lacking in the character of the girl; it showed that malicious, if rather low and vulgar, cunning which prompted the whole of this adventure; and it betrayed a revenge which was worthy of a Frenchwoman. Maclaren had but to hear the harsh ring of the voice to know that the girl who had threatened him months ago in New York had met her opportunity, and that she would use it to the last possibility. Every word that she uttered with such meaning vehe-

mence cut him like a knife; his hair glistened with the
drops of perspiration upon it; his right hand was passed
over his forehead as though some heat was tormenting
his brain. And as her voice rose shrilly, only to be
modulated to the pretence of suavity again, he blurted
out,—

"Evelyn, what are you going to do?"

"I—my dear Lord Maclaren—I am entirely in your
hands; you are my guest, I reckon, and even in America
we have some idea of what that means. Now, would
you like to play cards after dinner, or shall we have a
little music?"

The steward entered the cabin at this moment, and
the conversation being interrupted, Maclaren chanced to
see that the companion was free. A wild idea of appeal-
ing to the captain of the yacht came to him, and he made
a sudden move to mount the ladder. He had but taken
a couple of steps, however, when a lusty young fellow,
perhaps of twenty-five years of age, barred the passage,
and pushed him with some roughness into the cabin
again. The man closed the long, panelled door behind
him; and then addressed the unwilling guest.

"Ah, Maclaren, so that's you—devilish good of you to
come aboard, I must say."

The new-comer was Evelyn Lenox's brother, the
owner of the ketch *Bowery*. He acted his part in the
comedy with more skill than his sister, having less
personal interest in it; indeed, amusement seemed rather
to hold him than earnestness. It was perfectly
clear to Maclaren, however, that he would stand no
nonsense; and seeing that a further exhibition of feeling
would not help him one jot, the unhappy prisoner succumbed. When the dinner was put upon the table, he
found himself sitting down to it mechanically, and as

one in a dream. It was an excellent meal to come from
a galley; and it was made more appetising by the wit
and sparkle of the girl who presided, and who acted her
rôle to such perfection. She seemed to have forgotten
her anger, and cloaked her malice with consummate art.
She was a well-schooled flirt—and her victim consoled
himself with the thought, "They will put me ashore in
the morning, and I can make a tale." By ten o'clock he
found himself laughing over a glass of whisky and soda.
By eleven he was dreaming that he stood at the altar in
the church of St. Peter's, and that two brides walked up
the aisle together.

     *   *   *   *   *   *

The next picture that I have to show you of Maclaren
is one which I am able to sketch from a full report of
certain events happening on the evening of his wedding
day. The yacht lay becalmed some way out in the bay
of the Somme; the sea had the lustre of a mirror, golden
with a flawless sheen of brilliant light which carried
the dark shadows of smack-hulls and flapping lug-sails.
There was hardly a capful of wind, scarce an intermittent breath of breeze from the land; and the crew of
the *Bowery* lay about the deck smoking with righteous
vigour, as they netted or stitched, or indulged in those
seemingly useless occupations which are the delight of
sailors. Often, however, they stayed their work to listen
to the rise and fall of sounds in the saloon aft; and once,
when Maclaren's voice was heard almost in a scream,
one of them, squirting his tobacco juice over the bul-
warks, made the sapient remark; "Well, the old cove's
dander is riz now, anyway."

The scene below was played vigorously. Evelyn
Lenox sat upon the sofa, her arms resting upon the cabin
table, her bright face positively alight with triumph.

Maclaren stood before her with clenched hands and nashing teeth. Arthur, the brother, was smoking a pipe and pretending to read a newspaper, leaving the conversation to his guest, who had no lack of words.

"Good God, Evelyn," he said, "you cannot mean to keep me here any longer—to-morrow's my wedding day!"

She answered him very slowly.

"How interesting! I remember the time, not so long ago, when my wedding day was fixed—and postponed."

He did not heed the rebuke, but continued cravenly,—

"You do not seem to understand that your brother and yourself have perpetrated upon me an outrage which will make you detested in every country in Europe. Great Heaven! the whole town will laugh at me. I shan't have a friend in the place; I shall be cut at every club, as I'm a living man."

The girl listened to him, her eyes sparkling with the excitement of it. "Did you never stop to think," said she, "when you left America, like the coward you were, that people would laugh at me, too, and I should never be able to look my friends in the face again? Why, even in the newspapers they held me up to ridicule when my heart was breaking. You speak of suffering; well, I have suffered."

Her mood changed, as the mood of women does—suddenly. The feminine instinct warred against the actress, and prevailed. She began to weep hysterically, burying her head in her arms; and a painful silence fell on the man. He seemed to wait for her to speak; but when she did so, anger had succeeded, and she rose from her place and stamped her foot, while rage seemed to vibrate in her nerves.

"Why do I waste my time on you?" she cried; "you

who are not worth an honest thought. Pshaw! Lord Maclaren, illustrious nobleman and great sportsman "— she was quoting from an American paper—"go and tell them that for ten days you have humbled yourself to me, and have begged my pity on your knees. Go and tell them that my crew have held their sides when the parts have been changed, and you have been the woman. Oh, they shall know, don't mistake that; your wife shall read it on her wedding tour. I will send it to her my‑ self, I, who have brought the laugh to my side now, scion of a noble house. Go, and take the recollection of your picnic here as the best present I can give to you."

I was told that Maclaren looked at her for some moments in profound astonishment when she pointed to the cabin door. Then, without a word, he went on deck, to find the yacht's boat manned, and waiting for him. He said himself that many emotions filled him as he stepped off the yacht—anger at the outrage, desire for revenge, but chiefly the emotion of the thought, Was there time to reach St. Peter's for the wedding cere‑ mony? He did not doubt that lies would save him from the American woman, if things so happened that he could reach England by the morning of the next day. But could he? Where was he? Where was he to be put ashore? He asked the men at the oars these ques‑ tions in a breath, standing up for one moment as the boat pushed off to shake his fist at the yacht, and cry, " D—n you all!" But the answer that he got did not reassure him. He was to be put ashore, the seaman said, at Crotoy, the little town on a tongue of land in the bay of the Somme. There was a steamer thence once a day to Saint Valery, from which point he could reach Boulogne by rail. He realized in a moment that

K

all his hope depended on catching the steamer. If she had not sailed, he would arrive at Boulogne before sunset, and, if need were, could get across by the night mail and a special train from Folkestone. But if she had sailed! This possibility he dared not contemplate.

The men were now rowing rapidly towards the shore, whose sandy dunes and flat outlines were becoming marked above the sea-line. The yacht lay far out, drifting on a glassy mirror of water; the sun was sinking with great play of yellow and red fire in the arc of the west. Maclaren had then, however, no thought for Nature's pictures, or for seascapes. One burning anxiety alone troubled him—had the steamer sailed? He offered the men ten, twenty, fifty, a hundred pounds if they would catch her. The remark of one of them that she left on the top of the tide begot in him a mad eagerness to learn the hour of high-water; but none of those with him could remember it. He found himself swaying his body in rhythm with the oars as coxswains do; or standing up to look at the white houses shorewards. Another half-hour's rowing brought him a sight of the pier; he shouted out with a laugh that might have come from a jackal when he saw that the steamer was moored against it, and that smoke was pouring heavily from her funnels.

"Men," he said, "if you catch that boat, I'll give you two hundred and fifty pounds!" and later on their lethargy moved him to such disjointed exclamations as "For the love of heaven, get on to it!" "Now, then, a little stronger—fine fellows, all of you—a marriage depends upon this." "I'll give you a gold watch apiece, as I'm alive." "By ——, she's moving—no, she isn't, there's time yet, if you'll put your backs on to it—time, time—oh lord, what a crawl, what a cursed crawl!"

If one had peered into the faces of the yachtsmen
critically, one might have detected the ripples of smirks
about their lips; but Maclaren could not take his eyes
away from the steamer, and the import of the suppressed
amusement was lost upon him. The little town of Crotoy,

"MEN," HE SAID, "IF YOU CATCH THAT BOAT, I'LL GIVE YOU
TWO HUNDRED AND FIFTY POUNDS."

with the garish *établissement des bains*, the picturesque
church, and the time-wrecked ramparts escarped by the
ceaseless play of currents, was then not half a mile
away ; but a bell was ringing on the pier, and there was

all the hurry and the press known in "one packet" or
"one train" towns. Those who had much to do did it
slowly, that they might enjoy leisure to blow whistles or
to shout; those who had little atoned by great displays
of ineffective activity. Some ran wildly to and fro near
the steamer; others bawled incomprehensible ejacula-
tions, and incited, both those who were to leave by the
ship, and those who were not, to hurry, or they would
be late. Presently the little passenger steamer whistled
with a hoarse and lowing shriek, and cast foam behind her
wheels. Maclaren observed the motion, and cried out as
a man in pain, waving his arms wildly. Those on shore
mistook as much as they could see of his surprising
signals for a parting salute to the vessel; and she left
ten minutes after her time—without him.

He was hot from the battle of excitement, rivulets of
perspiration trickling upon his face; but he had breath
to curse the crew of the yacht's boat for five minutes
when he stepped ashore; and the request of the coxswain
to drink his health stirred up uncounted gifts for oath-
making within him. In a quarter of an hour he was
raving about the town of Crotoy, threatening to do himself injury if a boat were not forthcoming to carry him
to Saint Valery, whence he could get train to Boulogne.
But the day was nigh gone, and the local seamen were
at their homes. Few cared for his commission, and the
man who took it ultimately set him down just twenty
minutes after the last train had left.

*   *   *   *   *   *

The accounts given in the society papers for the aban-
donment of the wedding between Lord Maclaren and the
Hon. Christine King were many. The true one is found
in the simple statement that his Lordship did not reach
England until the evening of the day which had been fixed

for the ceremony. So the presents were returned—and I kept the pearls which were to have made the famous anchor bracelet. And when I think the matter over, I cannot wonder at Maclaren's hatred of them, or of his wish that I should burn them.

"Sutton," he said, "I was more than a fool. I ought to have remembered that Evelyn Lenox was with me when I saw the piece of stuff similar to that I wanted you to make. Why, I got the very notion of it from her, and it was only when one of your idiots let a society journalist know what you were doing for me that she heard of the marriage, and of my being at Ramsgate."

But the rest of his remarks were purely personal.

THE WATCH AND THE SCIMITAR

THE WATCH AND THE SCIMITAR

THE city of Algiers, the beautiful El Djzaïr, as the guide-book maker calls it, has long ceased to charm the true son of the East, *blasé* with the nomadic fulness of the ultimate Levant, or charged with those imaginary Oriental splendours which are nowhere writ so large as in the catalogues and advertisements of the later day upholsterer. This is not the fault of the new Icosium, as any student of the Moorish town knows well ; nor is it to be laid to the account of the French usurpation, and that strange juncture of Frank and Fatma, which has brought the boulevard to the city of the Corsairs and banished Mohammed to the shadow of the Kasbah. Rather, it is the outcome of coupons and of co-operative enthusiasm, which sends the roamer to many lands, of which he learns the names, and amongst many people with whose customs he claims familiarity.

To know Algiers, something more than a three days' *pension* in the Hôtel de la Régence is necessary ; though that is the temporal limit for many who return to Kensington or Mayfair to protest that " it is so French, you know." I can recollect well the monitions and advice which I received two years gone when I ventured a voyage to Burmah—in the matter of the ruby interest —and determined to see Cairo, Tunis, and the City of Mosques on my return westward. Many told me that I would do better to reach Jaffa and Jerusalem, others advised the seven churches of Asia; many spoke well of Rhodes; all agreed, whether they had been there or whether they had not, that Algiers was eaten up with Chauvinism, and scarce worthy a passing call. Baris-broke at the club, who is always vigorous in persuading other people not to do things, summed it up in one of his characteristically inane jokes. " It's had its Dey," said he, and buried himself in his paper as though the pro-ject ended then and there upon his own *ipse dixit.* This marked and decided consensus of opinion could have had but one result—it sent me to the town of Hercules at the first opportunity.

If the truth is to be told, the visit was in some part one of pleasure, but in the more part a question of sequins. I had done well in the remoter East, and had sent some fine parcels of rubies, sapphires, and pearls to Bond Street; but a side-wind of curiosity casting me up upon the shores of Tunis, I had bought there, in the house of a very remarkable Jew, a bauble whose rival in strange workmanship and splendour of effect I have not yet met with. It was, to describe it simply, the model of a Moorish scimitar perhaps four inches long, the sheath exquisitely formed of superb brilliants, the blade itself of platinum, and in the haft not only a strange medley of stones, but a little watch with a thin sheet of very fine pearl for a face, and a superb diamond as the cup of the hands. Although the jewels in this were worth perhaps five hundred pounds, the workmanship was so fine, and the whole bauble had such an original look, that I paid eight hundred pounds for it cheerfully, and thought myself lucky to get it at that. What is more to the point, however, is the fact that the hazard which gave me the possession of the scimitar sent me also to Algiers to hunt there for like curiosities—and in the end brought me a large know-

BUYING THE SCIMITAR.

ledge of the Moorish town, and nearly cost me my life.

I had intended to stay in the town for three days, but on the very evening of my coming to the Hôtel d'Orleans in the Boulevard de la République, I met a French lieutenant of artillery, a man by name Eugene Chassaigne; an exceedingly pleasant fellow, and one who had some Arabic, but small appreciation of anything beyond the "to-day" of life. He laughed at my notion of buying anything in the upper city, and urged me not to waste time plodding in dirty bazaars and amongst still dirtier dealers. For himself, his one idea was to be *dans le mouvement*; but he brought me to know, on the second day of my visit, a singularly docile Moor, Sidi ben Ahmed by name; and told me that if I still persisted in my intention, the fellow would serve well for courier, valet, or in any office I chose to place him. And in this he spoke no more than the truth, as I was very soon to prove.

I have always thought when recalling this sheep-like Moor to my recollection, that the Prophet had done him a very poor turn in locating him so far away from the blessings of company promotion and rickety building societies. His face would have been his fortune at any public meeting; and as for thoroughness, his love of detail was amazing. Before I had been in his hands for twenty-four hours he knew me; being able to tell you precisely how much linen I carried, the number of gold pieces in my purse, my taste in fish and fruits, my object in coming to his country. And this was vexatious; for all the vendors of Benares ware fashioned in Birmingham, all the sellers of gaudy burnouses, the hucksters of the tawdriest carpets and the most flimsy scimitars, held a concert on the steps of the hotel every time I showed my face within twenty paces of the door. Sidi alone was immobile, stolid. "*Nom d'un chien*—they are *blagueurs* all," said he; and I agreed with him.

If these things troubled my man, the jewel I had purchased in Tunis troubled him still more. How he learned that I had it heaven alone could tell; but he did not fail to come to me at *déjeuner* each morning and to repeat with unfailing regularity the monition, " If Allah wills, the jewel is stolen." I used to tolerate this at first; but in the end he exasperated me; and upon the seventh morning I showed him the model and said emphatically, " Sidi, you will please to observe that Allah does not will the loss of the jewel—let us change the subject." He gave me no answer, but on the next morning I had from him the customary greeting—and the laugh was all upon his side, for the scimitar was gone.

I say that the laugh was with Sidi, but in very truth I do not believe that this worthy fellow ever laughed in his life. He possessed a stolid immobility of countenance that would have remained in repose even at the sound of the last trumpet. The intelligence which I conveyed to him, I doubt not with pathetic anger, and much bad language, moved him no more than the soft south wind moved the statue of the first Governor-General out by the mosque there. He examined my ravished bag with a provoking silence; muttered a few pessimistic sentences in Arabic; and then fell back upon the Koran and the platitudes of his prophet. If he had been an English-man, I should have suspected him without hesitation; but he bore such a character, he had been so long a servant of the hotel, he was by his very stolidity so much above doubt, that this course was impossible; and being unable to accuse him, I bade him take me to the nearest bureau of police, that I might satisfy my conscience with the necessary farce. This he did without a protest, but I saw that he looked upon me with a pitying gaze, as one looks upon a child that is talking nonsense.

Although I flatter myself that I concealed my annoyance under a placid exterior, this loss affected me more than I cared to tell. For one thing, the jewel was very valuable (I was certain that I could have obtained a thousand pounds for it in Bond Street); I was convinced, moreover, that I should hardly discover its fellow if I searched Europe through. During my stay at the Hôtel d'Orleans I had kept it locked in a well-contrived leather pouch in my travelling trunk; and as this pouch had been opened with my own keys it was evident that the thief had access to my bedroom during the night— a conclusion which led me to think again of this stolid Moor, and to declare that the case against him was singularly convincing. So strong, in fact, were my suspicions that I made it my first care to go to the *maître* of the hotel and to demand satisfaction from him with all the justifiable indignation which fitted the case. When he heard my tale, his face would have given Rembrandt a study.

"How?" said he. "Monsieur is robbed, and *chez-moi*?"

I repeated that I was, and told him that if he did not recover the bauble in twenty-four hours, consequences would follow which would be disastrous to his establishment. Then I asked him frankly about the Moor Sidi; but he protested with tears in his eyes that he would as soon accuse his own mother. He did not deny that some one in his house might know something about it; and presently he had marshalled the whole of his servants in the central court, addressing them with the

fierce accusation of a *juge d'instruction*. It is super-
fluous to add that we made no headway, and that all
his "desolation" left me as far from the jewels I had
lost as I was at the beginning of it.

From the hotel to the bureau of the police was an easy
transition, but a very hopeless one. A number of extremely polite, and elaborately braided, officials heard
me with interest and pity; and having covered some
folios of paper with notes declared that nothing could
be done. For themselves, their theory was that the Moor
Sidi had been talking about my treasure, and that some
other domestic in the Hôtel de la Régence had opened my
door while I slept and got possession of the ornament
with little risk. But that any one should recover the
property was in their idea a preposterous assumption.

"It is on its way to Paris," said one of them as he
closed his note-book with a snap, "and there's an end of
it. We shall, without doubt, watch the servants of the
hotel closely for some time, but that should not encourage
you. It is possible that the man Mohammed, the porter
of the place, may know something of the affair. We
shall have his house searched to-day, but, my friend, *ne
vous montez pas la tête*, we are not in Paris, and the
upper town is worse than a beehive. I am afraid that
your hope of seeing the thing again is small."

I was afraid so, too; but being accustomed to strange
losses and to strange recoveries, I determined to venture
something in the hazard, and to remain in Algiers for a
few weeks, at any rate. The most difficult part of my
work lay in my ignorance of the city, and in that matter
Sidi alone could help me. Every day we went with
measured and expectant tread through that labyrinth of
fantastic and half-dark streets, where repulsive hags

grin at the wickets below, and dark eyes coquette at the gratings above; every day we delved in booths and bazaars, we haggled with the jewel sellers, we bartered with the gold workers, but to no purpose. I had come to think at last that the loss was not worth further trouble; and had made up my mind to return to London, when I recollected with some self-reproach that I had as yet neglected one of the very simplest means to grapple with the occasion—that I had, in fact, offered no reward for the recovery of the jewelled scimitar, and to this omission owed, I did not doubt, the utter absence of clue or conviction.

When I was yet angry with myself at this absurd oversight I had a second thought which was even more useful, and one to which I owed much before I had done with the matter. I remembered that the French police had set down my loss to the loud talk of Sidi amongst the others at the hotel. Why, then, I asked, should not this man also scatter the tidings that I would give so many hundreds of francs for the recovery of the scimitar? No sooner had I got the idea than I acted upon it.

"Sidi," said I, when he came to me on the next morning, "I have heard much of your cleverness, but you have not yet found my property; now I will give a thousand francs to the man who brings it here within a week."

To my utter surprise he bowed his head with his old gravity, and answered, "If Allah wills, the jewel is found."

This was amazing, no doubt, and in its way a triumph of impudence. If he could find it with that ease, then he must have known by whom it was stolen. I turned upon him at once with the accusation, but he stood with

the gravity of granite and responded to all my threats
with the simple greeting, as of a father to a son,—

"And upon you be peace."

To have argued with such a rogue would have been as
useful as a demonstration in theology before a mollah;

"'IF ALLAH WILLS, THE JEWEL IS FOUND.'"

to have accused him boldly of the theft would have been
absurd, even had I not possessed such a wealth of testi-
mony in his favour. I sent him about his business,
therefore, and went in search of my friend Chassaigne,
who had been away since I lost the trinket, but
was then at the arsenal again. The lieutenant took the

L

news with edifying calmness, but assured me that I had at last taken the only course which was at all likely to result in success.

"Our friend, the Moor," said he, "is the most honourable of his kind in Algiers, where all are rogues. I do not believe for a moment that he stole the jewels, although his father, his uncle, or his own brother may have done so. Your reward may tempt him to return them if the police set up a hue and cry; but if he suggests that you go up in the old town to receive them, tell him you will do nothing of the sort. There are far too many dark eyes and sharp knives there for an Englishman's taste, and a Moor still has claims in Paradise for every Frank he sticks. If you took the other course, and sought your money from this hotel-keeper, he would bring a hundred to swear that you did not lose the stones in the hotel, and you would be where you are. It's annoying to adopt a *laissez aller* policy, but I fear you can do nothing else."

I thought that he was right, but my habitual obstinacy was all upon me, and I found myself as much determined to recover the jewels I had lost as if they had been worth ten thousand pounds. I was quite sure that the police would do nothing, and save that they informed me in a cumbrous document that they had searched the house of Mohammed the porter, and of five others, my surmise proved a true one. It was left to Sidi, and for Sidi I waited on the morning of the ninth day with an expectancy which was unwarrantably large. He came to me at his usual hour, eight o'clock, and when he had salaamed, he said,—

"If Allah is willing, the jewel is found—but the money is not enough."

"Not enough!" said I, choking almost with anger,

"the money is not enough! Why, you brazen-faced blackguard, what do you mean?"

He replied with an appeal to the beard of the Prophet, and an evident word of contempt for my commercial understanding. The irony of the whole situation was so great, and his immobility so stupendous, that I quickly forbore my anger and said,—

"Very well, Sidi, we will make it fifteen hundred francs." And with that he went off again, and I saw him no more until the next day, when he repeated the *incha Allâh* and the intimation that the price was too low. On this occasion my anger overcame me. I seized him by the throat, and shaking him roughly, said,—

"You consummate rascal, I believe you have the jewels all the time; if you don't bring them in an hour, I will take you to the police myself."

My anger availed me no more than my forbearance. It did but awaken that inherent dignity, before which I cowed; and when I had done with him, he left me and came no more for three days. On the third morning when he returned he looked at me with reproach marked in his deep black eyes; and raising his hands to heaven he protested once more in the old words, and to the old conclusion. I was then so wearied of the very sound of his voice that I took him by the shoulders and held him down upon an ottoman until he would consent to bargain with me, shekel by shekel, for the return of my gems; and in the end he consented to make me the longest speech that I had yet had from his lips.

"By the beard of my father," said he, "I protest to milord that neither I nor my people have the precious thing he wots of; but the dog of a thief, upon whose head be desolation, is known to me. For money he took the jewel, for money he shall lay it again at milord's feet;

yet not here, but in the house of his people, where none shall see and none shall know."

A long argument, and some fine bargaining, enabled me to get to the bottom of the whole story; but only under a solemn oath that the keeping of the secret should be shared by no one. With much fine recital and many appeals to the holy marabouts to bear witness, Sidi demonstrated that the thief was no other than Mohammed the porter, who had the stone hidden with extraordinary cunning, and from whom it was to be got only at my own personal risk.

"Under the shadow of the Kasbah it lies," said he; "under the shadow of the Kasbah must you seek it with those I shall send to you, and no others. Obey them in all things; be silent when they are silent, speak when they speak, fly and lose not haste when they bid you fly."

This was all very vague, but a deeper acquaintance with his purpose made it the more clear. In answer to my question why he could not bring the jewel to the hotel, he said that it would never be surrendered except to a certain force; and with that force he would supply me. He himself seemed to be under an oath to bear no hand to the emprise; and he was emphatic in laying down the condition that I must go absolutely alone; or, said he, "the hand of Fatma shall not be passed nor that which you seek come to you."

Now, the proper spirit in which to have received this suggestion would have been that of an uncompromising negative. Chassaigne had cautioned me particularly against going into the old town, and here was I hearkening to a proposition to visit it not only by night, but in the company of those who possibly were honest, but more possibly were cut-throats. I knew well enough what he would say to the venture; and truly I was much disposed to refuse it at the beginning, and to go to London as I had at first intended. This I told Sidi, and he gave me for answer a shrug of the shoulders, which implied that if I did, my property, for which I hoped to get a thousand pounds, would certainly remain behind me. Nor did threats and entreaties move him one iota from his position, neither on that day nor on the next two; so that I saw in the end that I had better decide quickly, or take ship and fly a city of indolent Frenchmen and rascally Moors.

It would prove tedious to recount to you the various processes of reasoning by which, finally, I found myself of a mind to court this hazard and agreed to Sidi's terms. He on his part had vouched for my safety; and after all, the man who ever wraps his life in cotton-wool, as it were, must see little beyond the stuffy box on his own habitation. Here was a chance to see the Moors *chez-eux*, possibly to risk a broken head with them; in any case, a chance which an adventurous man might be thankful for, and which I took.

Having once agreed to Sidi's terms, he set upon the realization of the project with unusual ardour. The very next evening was chosen for the undertaking, the hour being close upon ten, and the Moor himself accompanying me some part of the way. He had advised me to equip myself *en Arabe* for the business; and this I did with some little discomfort, especially in the manipulation of the long burnouse, and in the carriage of appalling headgear which he would not allow me to dispense with. I had put these things on at the hotel; but as it is not unusual for a Frank to ape the Moor when wishing to explore the upper town at night, I escaped unpleasant curiosity, and arrived at the steep ascent of the Rue de la Lyre, feeling that I was like, at any rate, to get more excitement out of the old city than nine-tenths of the Englishmen who visit her.

Almost at the top of the street the Moor's friends met me. I could see little of their faces, for they covered them as much as possible with their sombre-hued cloaks, but they salaamed profoundly on greeting me; and Sidi took his leave when he had exchanged a few words in Arabic with them. From that time onward they did not speak, but went straight forward into the old quarter; and soon we had entered a narrow way where flights of stairs, frequently recurring, led one up towards the Kasbah. Here the gables seemed to be exchanging whispered confidences as they craned forwards across the stone-paved ascent; you could see the zenith of the silver sky shot with starlight through the jutting angles of rickety roofs and bulging eaves; the hand of Fatma protected the hidden doors of the pole-shored but singularly picturesque houses; the sound of tom-toms and *derboukas* came from the courts of the Kahouaji. The peace of the scene, deriving something from the distant and seductive harmonies, got colour from the slanting flood of moonlight which streamed upon the pavement, from the swell of song floating upward from the hidden courts. Here and there one imagined that black eyes looked down upon one from the gratings of the shadowed windows above; a Biskri, strong of limb and bronzed, lurked now and then in the dark angles of the quaint labyrinth; a few Moors passing down to the lower city inclined their heads gravely as we passed them. But for the most part the children of the Prophet had gone to their recreations or their sleep; the narrow path of stairs was untenanted; the silence and softness of an African night held sway with all its potent beauty.

We must have mounted for ten minutes or more
before my guides stopped at a large house in a particularly uninviting looking *cul-de-sac* ; and having spoken
a few words with an old crone at the wicket, we gained
admittance to a large court, and found it packed with
a very curious company. It was a picturesque place, .
gloriously tiled, and surrounded by a gallery supported
on slender columns of exquisite shape, terminating in
Moorish arches and fretwork balustrades. There the
women, numbering some score, sat; but I, knowing the
danger of betraying the faintest interest in a Moor's
household, averted my eyes at once, and examined more
minutely the strange scene below. Here was a dense
throng surrounding a dervish who danced until he
foamed ; a throng of bronzed and bearded Arabs sipping
coffee and smoking hubble-bubble pipes with profound
gravity; a throng which seemed incapable of expressing
any sort of emotion, either of pleasure or of pain. At
the further end of the court, where many luxuriant
palms and jars of gorgeous flowers gave ornament to a
raised daïs, musicians squatted upon their haunches,
playing upon divers strange instruments, guitars, flutes,
and the gourd-like *derbouka*, and sent up a hideous and
unbroken wave of discordant harmony which made the
teeth chatter and seemed to agitate one's very marrow.
It was a strange scene, full of life and colour, and above
all of activity ; and to what it owed its origin I have
not learnt to this day. I know only that our coming
with such a lack of ceremony did not disconcert either
the host or his guests. They paused a moment to give
us an " Es-salaam âlikoum," to which we returned the
expected " Oua âlikoum es-salaam "; and with that we
sat amongst the company, but in a very conspicuous
place, and took coffee with the gravity of the others.

I must confess that the surprise of finding myself in
such a place was very great. I had gone with the
Moors to recover a thousand pounds' worth of property,
but how the visit brought me nearer to that, or to any
purpose whatever, I could not see. I knew that I was
the only European in the company, and all tradition as
well as common-sense told me of my danger. Yet I had
gone of my own will, and the Moor Sidi had encouraged
me to the risk, which after all, I thought, was worth
bartering for the sight of so strange an entertainment.
Indeed, it is not in accord with my fatalistic creed to
conjure up terrors of the mind in moments of comparative tranquillity; and when I realized that the question
of wisdom, or want of wisdom, was no longer under
discussion, I fell in with the spirit of this singular
festivity—and waited for enlightenment.

The feast of performance was now going briskly. A
conjurer trod upon the heels of the dervish, and per-
formed a few palpable feats which deceived no one but
himself; and after that we had the expected dancing
girls, and the Ouled-Naïls. Nor were the latter the
central piece, as it were, of our host's programme; for
presently the Moors about me ceased their babbling;
there was a restless chatter in the gallery above, the
old host whispered something to his attendant, and new
musicians, who had relieved the others, struck up a
hideous banging of tom-toms, flageolets, and guitars.
At that very moment, when I had come to the conclusion that Sidi ben Ahmed had made a fool of me, and
that my errand was to end idly, one of my guides spoke
for the first time, putting his mouth close to my ear,
and using very passable English. "Now," said he, "be
ready"; but whether he meant me to prepare for some
saltatory display, or for action, he did not condescend

to say; and before I could ask him a great applause greeted the advent of a dancing girl, who bounded into the arena with a conventional run, and at once began her amazing gyrations.

She was a beautiful girl, not more than eighteen years of age, I should think, and probably a Circassian. She had clear-cut features, a complexion bright with the freshness of youth, a figure of fine balance and maturity; but the most striking thing about her was her hair. More abundant or glossier tresses I have never seen. In colour, a deep golden-red, this magnificent silky gift was bunched upon her head in a great coil at the back, and fell thence almost to her feet. It covered her when she chose as the burnouses covered the Moors who watched her; and she used it in her dancing with a *chic* and skill unimaginable. In one moment coiling it about her body so that she seemed wrapped in a sheen of gold; in the next cast like an outspread fan behind her, she presented a picture ravishing beyond description, and one which drew shouts of "Zorah, Zorah!" even from the women in the galleries above. I sat under the spell, enraptured like the rest; and as the girl floated with a dreamy lightness, or pirouetted with amazing agility, or swept past me with a motion that was the very essence of grace, I was ready to declare that the dance was unrivalled by anything I had seen in any of the capitals.

Now, the girl must have been dancing for a couple of minutes, and the audience was thoroughly held by her prodigious cleverness, when I, engrossed as the others, was suddenly interrupted in my contemplation of her by the action of the Moors, my guides. To my utter surprise they of a sudden stood up on either side of me, and one of them crying to me in English as

before to be ready, the other seemed to wait for the girl
Zorah, who, with streaming hair and body thrown well
back, was dancing down towards us.

A few of the company near to us turned their heads,
and cried out at the interruption; but the girl came on
with quick steps, and when she was just upon us, the
Moor who waited seized her by her hair, and putting
his hands in the great coil upon her head, he unrolled
it with a strong grasp, and the missing scimitar, to
my unutterable surprise, rolled out upon the pavement.

I am willing to confess that for one moment the whole
action dazed me so completely that I stood like a fool
gaping at the jewel, and at the girl, who had begun to
cling to the Moor and to scream. The thing was so
unlooked for, so strange, so incredible, that I could do
nothing but ask myself if it were really my bauble that
lay upon the floor, or was I the victim of an incomprehensible trick? Yet there was the jewel, and there at
my elbow were the two Moors, now all ready for the
action aftermath. Scarce, in fact, had one of them
picked up my property and crammed it into my hand
before the uproar began, the whole roomful of erstwhile
sedate-looking men springing to their feet and turning
upon us. For an instant, the Moor who had snatched
the jewel for me kept them back with an harangue in
Arabic of which I did not understand one word; but his
best and only card failed him at the first playing, and
it remained to face the danger and to fight it.

Of the extraordinary scene that followed I remember
but little. It seemed to me that I was surrounded in an
instant by hungry, gleaming, hawk-like eyes which
glowed with mischief; that women screamed, that
lamps were overturned; that I saw knives flashing on

every side of me. Had Sidi's men then failed him or
displayed any craven cunning, I take it that my body
might have been hurled from the Kasbah within a
minute of the recovery of the jewel; but they showed

"THE GIRL FLOATED WITH A DREAMY LIGHTNESS."

quite an uncommon fidelity and courage. Standing on
either side of me so that my body was almost wedged
between theirs, they suddenly flashed long knives in the
air, and cut and parried with wondrous dexterity. For

myself, I had only my fists, and these I used with a
generous freedom, thinking even in the danger that a
Moor's face is a substantial one to hit; and that a little
boxing goes a long way with him.   Yet I could not help
but realize that the minute was a supreme one, and as the
crowd of demoniacal and shouting figures pressed nearer
and nearer, threatening to bear us down in the *mêlée*,
I heard my heart thumping, and began to grow giddy.

As the press became more furious, the two men who
had done so well were gradually carried away from me.
I found myself at last in the lower corner of the room,
surrounded by four burly fellows (the main body of the
company swarming round the Moors, my guides); and
of these but one had a knife in his hand.   With this,
taking the aggressive, he made a prodigious cut at me,
which slit my left arm from the shoulder almost to the
elbow; but I had no pain from the wound in the excitement of the moment; and I sent him howling like a
dervish with a heavy blow low down upon the chest.
Of the others, one I hit on the chin, whereupon he cried
like a woman; but the remaining two sprang upon me
with altogether an unlooked for activity; and bore me
down with a heavy crash upon the pavement.   I thought
then that the end had come; for not only was I half
stunned with the blow, but the man who knelt upon
my chest gripped my throat with grim ferocity and
threatened to squeeze the life out of me as I lay.   In
that supreme moment I recollect that the lights of the
room danced before my eyes in surprising shapes; that
I saw a vision of dark-eyed but screaming women in
the gallery above; that the jewel in my vest cut my
skin under the pressure of the Moor's knee; and that
I fell to wondering if I would live one minute or five.
Then, as a new and violent shouting reached me, even

above the singing in my ears, the Moor suddenly let go his hold, the light of the scene gave way to utter impenetrable darkness, and I fainted.

* * * * * *

Next day I took *déjeuner* at the Café Apollon with my arm in a sling, and Chassaigne's talk to whet my appetite. He had occupied himself during the morning in cross-examining Sidi, from whom he had wormed the whole secret of the robbery.

"It is as clear as the sun," said he, "the porter Mohammed was advised to steal the jewel by the man I unfortunately recommended to you. Mohammed, knowing that the police would search his house and watch him, hid the jewel in his wife's hair."

"His wife !" said I. "Was this dancing girl married to a scamp like that ?"

"Certainly; these Circassians don't make great matches, if they make a good many of them. Their husbands are generally loafers about the cafés; and this girl was no more fortunate in that way than most of her sisters. You see, the fun of the business is that Sidi got two thousand francs from this man for telling him how to steal your jewels, and another two thousand from you for stealing them back again. That's why he did not go with you himself last night. Luckily, I went into your hotel at ten o'clock, and learning from the man where you had gone, I followed you with a dozen of my fellows."

"You came at a happy time, my dear fellow," said I, "in another five minutes I should have needed only an executor."

"That's true; you were nearly dead when I had the pleasure of kicking the man who sat on your head. But it was your own fault, you must admit."

"Any way," said I, "I got the stones, and that's something."

He agreed to this, and when I had thanked him for the great service he had done me, we parted. That night I left Algiers, carrying with me the pacific benediction of the admirable Moor, Sidi, who, despite the fact that I had kicked him down the steps of the hotel in the morning, came with me to the steamer, and patronised me to the end of it. I can hear to this day his last and final salutation :—

"Blessed be Allah, the jewel is found !"

THE SEVEN EMERALDS

THE SEVEN EMERALDS

THE man stood upon the weir-bridge watching me; a conspicuous man with strange clothes for river-work upon him, and a haunting activity which drove him from the lock to the inn, and again from the inn to the lock with a crazy restlessness which was maddening. I had been for some hours whipping the mill-stream, which lies over against the lockhouse at Pangbourne; but meeting with no success amongst the chub, which on this particular July evening were aggravatingly indifferent even to the succulent frog, I had punted to the bushes in the open river; and there lit my pipe and fell to speculation upon him who favoured me with so close an attention. I have said that he was a conspicuous man, and to this I owed it that I had seen him. He wore the straw hat of Jesus College, Cambridge, and a velvet coat which shone brown and greasy in the falling sunlight; but his legs were encased in salmon-pink riding breeches, and he had brown boots reaching to his knees. Beyond this, he was singularly handsome, so far as I could judge with the river's breadth between us; and his hair was fair with a ridiculous golden strain quite unlooked for in one who has grown to manhood. Why he watched me so closely I could not even conjecture, but the fact was not to be disputed. I had lain by the mill since the forenoon, and since the forenoon he had hugged to the weir-bridge or to the lockhouse, giving no attention to the score of small boats and launches which passed up or down to Goring or Mapledurham; or even to the many pretty women who basked upon the cushions of punts or pair-oars. I alone was the object of his gaze, and for me he seemed to wait through the afternoon and until the twilight.

Now, had the man hailed me, I should have gone shorewards at once, for my curiosity had been petted by his attentions until it waxed warm and harassing; but this he did not do; keeping his eyes upon me even when I had rested from casting and sat idling in the punt. It would have been easy, I concede, to have gone up river toward Goring and so to have avoided him; but this would have cut short the chance of explanation, and have left ungratified my desire to know who he was, and wherefrom came his embarrassing interest in my failure to ensnare the exasperating chub. So I sat there, in turn wondering if he were honest or a rogue, an adventurer or an idler, a river-man or a fop from Piccadilly. And as the problem was beyond me, I left it at last; and taking up my punt-pole I gave three or four vigorous thrusts which sent me immediately to the landing-stage of the Swan Inn, and thence to my room.

It may be urged that this was an indifferent way of dealing with the man in the velvet coat if I wished to know more of him; but I had taken that little parlour of the inn which juts out upon the hard of the boathouse; and I could see from my open windows both the panorama of the lock and that of the open reach away towards the islands. It was now close upon the hour of seven, and the most part of the river lay in cooling shadow. I could hear by no means inharmonious music floating out over the water from a girl's guitar; there were several launches waiting for the lock-gates; and I recall well the face of a very remarkable woman, who presently came to the landing-stage in a gig, the cushions of which were of an aggressive yellow, but one which was a striking contrast to her black hair and ivory-white skin. Quite apart, however, from her indisputable beauty, I had reason to watch this conspicuous oars-woman, for no sooner had she come to the landing-stage than the man in the velvet coat went to her assistance, and taking a number of bags and baskets from the boat, accompanied her up the village high street, and so carried her from my view.

Here then, thought I, is the end of my mystery. The man had been waiting for the return of his wife, when I, with preposterous conceit, plumed myself that he had been looking to speak with me. What creatures of ideas we are! And when I reflected upon it, certainly it was monstrous absurd to think that one man should wish to watch another failing to catch fish through a long summer's afternoon. Indeed, I laughed heartily at myself as the maid set my dinner, and I put my creel and rod upon the piano (one puts everything upon the piano in a Thames village) before daring the very substantial, if rural, repast served to me.

One dines up river, as most people know, in semi-public state. Loafers, loiterers, fruit-sellers, boatmen— all these congregate near the open window, and discuss verbally the dishes which the diner discusses more substantially. Custom so stales us that this publicity in no way interferes with our pleasure. I have so long learned to tolerate the presence before my casement of oarsman, pedlar, and even the less welcome bargee, that these now are almost as salt to my appetite. And for the matter of that, on the evening of which I am writing, the crowd was less than usual, being composed of one

vendor of fruit, three men in obviously Cheapside
blazers, and an old woman who sold boot-laces and discussed the weather with me through the casement at one
and the same time. She was such a merry old soul, and
gave me so much of her history and of that of her son,
who was "fightin' for his Quane and counthry" in a
place which she could not mind herself of, that I forgot
the ridiculous romance of the velvet-coated man, and
even his existence, until of a sudden he presented himself, no longer watching me upon the bridge, but standing at the casement, and asking to be admitted.

"I'm most horribly sorry," said he, "to intrude upon
you at your dinner, but my train leaves for town in ten
minutes, and I particularly want your opinion upon
something which they tell me you know more about than
any man in England."

"By all means," said I. "But your estimate of my
opinion is hopelessly flattering; it concerns jewels, I
suppose?"

"Exactly," said he; "and I shall be under very large
obligations to you if you will tell me whether two
emeralds I have in my pocket are of any value, and if
so, where would be the best place to dispose of them?"

He took a little paper box from his coat, and laid it
near to my plate. I saw that it was a box which had
contained tabloids of nitro-glycerine (a drug prescribed
for diseases of the heart); and that it had been sold by a
chemist of the name of Benjamin Wain, whose shop was
in the High Street at Reading. These things I observed
with my intuitive habit of grasping detail, learnt in
long contention with rogues; and then forgot them as
the man opened a screw of tissue paper, and I beheld
two of the finest emeralds I have seen during my career.
The stones were perfectly matched, of a rich velvety,

but brilliant colour, and came, I did not doubt after my first sight of them, from the Upper Orinoco or from Columbia. Their weight I judged to be about five carats each, and I knew that if they were without a flaw, which very few emeralds are, they would be worth fifteen hundred pounds at a very low estimate. All this passed through my mind like a flash; but with admiration of the gems, which brought covetousness in its path, there came at once the other thought—what is this man doing here with these stones, and how comes it that he can carry them and yet be unconscious of their value? But this I endeavoured to conceal, and waited for him to speak.

"Well," said he, after a pause, "do you find much the matter with them?"

"I should want my glass to see," said I with caution; "the light is failing, and my eyes are not as good as they were."

"You mean a magnifying glass, I suppose?" said he, producing a lens from his pocket. "Well, I happen to have one."

Why it was I cannot tell you, but this trifling circumstance I marked down in my mind as my first sound cause of suspicion against him. Perhaps I coupled it with that spontaneous distrust which I felt when first he spoke, for the very softness of his voice was obviously assumed; and now that I saw him near to me, I did not fail to notice that the velvet coat was much worn, and the rowing club tie he wore frayed beyond respectability. But I took his lens, and, having examined the stones long and critically under it, I found them to be without flaw or blemish. Then I gave him my opinion.

"They are fine stuff," said I; "do you happen to know where they come from?"

I looked him full in the face when I spoke, and observed a slight drawing of the lines above his mouth. When he answered me I was sure that he had thought out a lie—and with effort.

"I believe they come from Salzburg," he stammered; "at least I have heard so."

"That could not possibly be," said I; "the worst emeralds we have are the best product of that mine. I fancy they are from Venezuela."

"Ah, that's the place," said he, "I remember it now; but I've a wretched head for geography."

While he said this the train to London steamed out of the railway station, which is not a stone's throw from the inn, and he, forgetful of his tale to me, sat watching it unconcernedly. I had discovered him in a second lie, and I waited to entrap him to a third with the practised pleasure of a cross-examiner.

"Do you sell these stones for yourself or as an agent?" I asked, assuming some authority as I felt surer of him. His hesitation in answering was merely momentary, but it was enough for my purpose.

"For myself," said he; and then with clumsy maladroitness he added, "They were left to me by my father, and I have never had the heart to offer them to any one. I'll tell you what, though; if you'll give me a thousand pounds for the pair, you shall keep them."

"That's a long price," said I; "and if you don't mind the suggestion, my dinner's getting cold."

I had spoken thus with the design of putting him off; but he was undisguisedly an ill-bred man, and I saw that I could have bought the emeralds from him for five hundred pounds. My hint—if such you could call it—fell upon deaf ears; and he, seeming not to hear it, con-

tinued to argle-bargle, but betraying himself in every
word he said.

"Come, now," he cried, "you don't want to be hard
upon me; give me a cheque for five hundred, and send

" HE ROSE UP SUDDENLY FROM HIS CHAIR, AND HAVING MADE A BUNGLING
PARCEL OF HIS JEWELS, WENT OFF BY HIMSELF."

the balance to Brighton in a week if you find them as
good as you think. That's a fair offer, isn't it?"

"The offer is fair enough," said I; "but you forget

that I did not come here to buy emeralds. I am in Pangbourne to catch chub, as you saw this afternoon."

"I'm afraid I can't agree to that," he replied with a laugh; "I did not see you catch chub this afternoon—I saw you miss three."

"The bait was poor," I said meaningly; "fish are as canny as men, and don't take pretty things if they think there's a hook in them."

This I gave him with such a stare that he rose up suddenly from his chair, and, having made a bungling parcel of his jewels, went off by himself. He had to pass my window as he left the inn, and as he crossed the road I called after him, saying,—

"You'll be losing your train to London."

"Be d——d to that!" said he; and with such a salute he turned the angle of the road, and I lost sight of him.

But I thought much of his emeralds through the night, both in my walk across the old wooden bridge to Whitchurch, when the river lay dark and gloomy with the sough of the breeze in the reeds and sedge-grass; and again as I lay in the old wooden "best-bed" of the inn, and contemplated the "sampler" which bore witness to the energy of one Jane Atkins, whose work it was. By what chance had the man found me out? Whence came his seedy clothes and his jewels? Who was the pretty woman who had gone up from the hard with him? He had come by the stones fraudulently, of course; had the case been different he would have sent them to London to a house of substance, and there got his price for them. At one time I felt that it lay upon me to advise the police in Reading of the offer I had received; at another, there came some regret for the stones, and at the manner of his departure. The season had been one of emeralds.

I could have sold the pair he had for some profit, and, as my greed told me, I could have bought them cheap. At the end of it I fell asleep to dream that I rowed to Mapledurham in an emerald boat, and that a man with emerald eyes steered me abominably.

On the next day, quite early in the morning, I set out in a dogcart for Reading, having a *rendezvous* with Barisbroke at the Kennet's mouth, whence we were to start for a day's sport upon that fish-breeding river. My drive took me by the old Bath-road, turning to the left midway up the village street; but I had not gone very far upon the Reading-road before I saw the handsome woman — the wife, as I assumed, of the velvet-coated man—now dressed with exceeding poorness, and carrying a heavy bag towards the biscuit town. At this point the sun beat early upon the sandy way with a shimmer of white and misty light, which promised great heat of the forenoon; there was scarce a quiver of wind in the woods to the left of me, and I did not doubt that walking was a great labour. Yet, when I reined-in the cob, and asked the woman, if at least I might not carry her bag to Reading and leave it for her, she thanked me somewhat curtly I thought, and evidently resented any notice of her difficulty. It occurred to me, as I drove on, that the man, who had been with her on the previous day, had really left by the last train for London; but when I came into Reading, and was about to cross the High Street, to reach Earleigh, I saw the name Benjamin Wain superscribed above a little chemist's shop, and I stopped at once. I know that a county tradesman will gossip like a fishwife; and I asked the man for some preparation which he could not possibly find in the pharmacopœia, and so began to feel my ground.

"You're well ahead of the times here," said I, looking at his show-case, which was woefully destitute of drugs. 'I shouldn't have thought that you'd be asked for tabloids in a place like Reading."

"Oh, but we are," said he readily; "it's a wonderfully advanced town is Reading—you won't get much in Regent Street which is not here. I've lived in Reading all my life—and seen changes, sir, indeed I have!"

"You know most of the people then?" said I, with a purpose.

"Ay," said he, "I've born and buried a many, so to speak; seen children grow to men and women, and men and women grow to children—you wouldn't think it perhaps!"

"No," said I, "you don't show it; but your reputation, if I may say so, goes beyond this place. I was in Pangbourne yesterday, where a tall, yellow-haired man was speaking of you; who is he, I wonder?"

"A tall, yellow-haired man!" he exclaimed, putting his finger in the centre of his forehead as if in aid of memory; "I didn't know there were such in Reading A tall, yellow—let me see, now——"

"You sold him some tabloids of nitro-glycerine; perhaps that will help to his identification?" said I.

"Ah, now I know you're wrong," said he; "there's only one man within five miles of here who uses that stuff, and he hasn't got yellow hair—ha, ha, he hasn't got any at all."

"Who is he?" I asked with growing curiosity.

"Why, old Jabez Ladd, the miser, out at Yore Park; he takes that stuff for his heart, sir. Wonderful weak heart he has, too; but he hasn't got yellow hair—no, I may say with conviction that he has no hair at all."

I had learnt all I needed, for the mere mention of the

name Jabez Ladd was sufficient for me. At the man's
words a whole freshet of ideas seemed to rush to my
mind. I had known the miser for years as one of the
hardest jewel buyers in the country; I had sold him
thousands of pounds' worth of stuff; I had heard the
strangest traditions of his astounding meanness and
self-denial. They even said that he forbade himself a
candle after dusk, and that his fare was oatmeal and
brown bread; while he lived in a house which would
not have been a poor retreat for a millionaire. This I
knew, but the words of the apothecary had made other
things clear to me—one, that the yellow-haired man had
got his emeralds in a box which must have come from
Ladd's house, since he alone in the neighbourhood took
tabloids of nitro-glycerine; another, that the man's very
shabbiness and obvious shuffling pointed very strongly
to the conclusion that he should be watched.

Of these things was I sure as I met Barisbroke, and I
turned them over in my mind often during the moderate
sport of the forenoon, and after. Not that I had any
troublesome friendship for Ladd, who was no sort of a
man to think about; yet I could not forget that he was
a buyer, and it seemed both wise and likely to be pro-
fitable to warn him. Possibly I had reared a fine
superstructure of suspicion upon a mere flimsy basis
of prejudice; but in any case I could do no harm, I
thought, and might even sell the old scoundrel a parcel
of jewels in the attempt. His house, as I then knew, lay
over by the hills of Caversham; and I remembered that
I could take it by a circuitous route which would bring
me to Pangbourne, after I had passed through Mapledurham and Whitchurch. In the end, I resolved at least
to see the old man; and when I had dined at a ridiculously early hour with Barisbroke, I crossed the river by

the white bridge, and in thirty minutes I was at the gate
of Yore Hall.

I am no archæologist, and have an exceedingly poor
eye for a building; but my first impression of this hall
was a pleasing one. It is true that the wooden gate of
the drive was broken down, and the garden-land beyond
it nothing but a tangle of swaying grass, thistle, and
undergrowth, preparing one for poor things to come;
but the house itself was a massive and even a grand
attempt at a towered and battlemented structure, built
in stout stone with Norman windows, and the pretence
of a keep, which gave strength to its air of antiquity.
When I came near to it, I saw that many of the gar-
goyles had fallen from the roof of the left wing, which
seemed to be unfinished, and the parapet was broken
away and decaying above the porch; while—and this
was even more singular—there did not seem a single
curtain to the house. It was now upon the hour of
seven, and a glimmer of sunlight shining redly upon the
latticed casements lit up the façade with a greater
brilliance than one looks to see out of Italy. There were
rooks circling and cawing in the great elms by the moat
which ran round three sides of the house; I could hear
the baying of a hound in the courtyard by the stables—
but of man or woman I saw nothing, though I rang the
great bell thrice, and birds fled from the eaves at the
clatter, and the rabbits that had sported by the thicket
disappeared in the warren.

Some minutes after the third ring, and when I was
preparing to drive off and leave Jabez Ladd to his own
affairs, the stable door opened, and a girl came out,
dressed, it seemed to me, curiously in a smart white
frock; but with untidy hair, though much of it; and an
exceedingly pretty face, which had been the prettier for

"'THERE'S NO NEED,' SAID SHE, SIMPERING AGAIN; 'HE'S BEEN A-BED
SINCE THE MILK.'"

a little scouring. The creaturè had great dark eyes like a *grisette* of Bordeaux; and when she saw me, stood swaying upon her feet, and laughing as she bit at her apron-strings, as though my advent was an exceedingly humorous thing. Then she said,—

" Is it Mr. Ladd you're wanting?"

I told her that it was.

" You'll not be a county man?" she asked.

" I'm from London," said I, " and my name is Bernard Sutton Tell Mr. Ladd that I'll not keep him five minutes."

" There's no need," said she, simpering again; " he's been a-bed since the milk."

" In bed!" cried I amazed.

" Yes," said she, " it's over late for company; but if ye'll write something I'll run up with it; the house-keeper's away sick."

She seemed to think that all this was a good joke, and wondered, I doubt not, that I did not simper at her again. I was on the very point of whipping up the nag, and leaving such a curious household, when one of the landing windows went up with a creak, and Ladd him-self, with a muffler round his throat, was visible.

" What d'ye want in my grounds?" he roared. ' Here, you hussy, what are ye chattering there for?— thought I was asleep did ye—ha!"

" Good evening, Mr. Ladd," said I, quietly; " I'm sorry, but I appear to have disturbed you. I've a word for your ear if you'll come down."

" Hullo," cried he, in his cracked and piercing voice; " why it's you, is it? egad, I thought you were the butcher! What's your business?—I'm biding in bed, as you can see."

" I can't shout," said I, " and my business is private."

" Won't it wait ? " he snarled. " You haven't come to
sell me anything ? "

"I don't sell stuff in the street," said I; "come down
and I'll talk to you. But if you don't want to hear—
well, go to bed."

His curiosity got the better of him at this point, and
he snapped out the words, "I'm coming down," and then
disappeared from the window. But he had no intention
of opening the front door, as I found presently, when of
a sudden he appeared at a casement upon the ground
floor, and resumed the conversation.

" You're not asking after my health," said he, " but
I'll let you know that I'm eat up with cold; can ye have
done with it straight off? "

" Yes," said I, leaning over from the dog-cart to spare
my voice. "Do you know a tall man with yellow hair
who's got two emeralds to sell ? "

At these words his face whitened in the sunlight, and
he opened his great mouth as though to speak, but no
sound came. Then quickly he drew a small box from
his pocket, such as I had seen in the hands of the velvet-
coated man, and took a tabloid from it.

" I'll be about letting you in," said he, as he went to
shut down the casement.

But I said, " I think not, there's a drive of five miles
to Whitchurch before me, and this horse trips."

"For the love of God," cried he, suddenly putting off
all self-restraint, "don't go till I've heard you—man, my
life may depend upon it ! "

" How's that ? " said I.

" I'm going to tell you," said he; "and if ye'll stay,
we'll crack a bottle of port together."

He had whetted my curiosity now, and presently I
heard him nagging at the pretty girl who had first

greeted me. After that he ·threw the stable door wide
open, and dressed only, as I could see, in a loose dress-
ing-gown and a pair of carpet slippers, he led the horse
to a stall that had the half of a roof; crying to the maid
to get her down to the house of a man he named, there
to beg a feed of corn and the loan of a boy. But while
he was doing it, he shivered incessantly, and seemed
eaten up with fear.

"You appear to think that I'm putting up with.you,"
said I, when I heard his orders; "there's no need to look
after the nag—I sha'n't be here ten minutes."

"Not ten minutes!" he exclaimed, still with quaver-
ing voice. "Oh, but you will—when you've heard my
talk. Would you see me murdered?"

I did not answer, being in the main amused at his
attempts to get the horse out of the trap, and particularly to unbuckle the very stiff belly-band. The girl
had gone tripping off with herself to the village as I
thought; but though at that time I had no intention of
staying beyond an hour with him, I unshafted the
animal myself, and tethered the beast to the rickety
manger, throwing my own rug across his loins; then I
followed Ladd through a black and smoke-washed
kitchen to a dingy apartment near the hall, and, the
place being shuttered, he kindled a common paraffin
lamp, which might have cost a shilling, but would have
been dear at two.

"I'll be getting the port," said he, casting a wistful
look at me in the hope, perhaps, that I should decline his
invitation to a glass, "you'll not mind refreshment after
your drive?"

"Thanks; you may be sure I won't," said I; and while
he was gone fumbling down the passage, I saw that his
dining-room had once been a fine apartment, oak-

panelled and spacious; and that ancestors, whose rubi-
cund jowls spoke of "two-bottle" men, now seemed
to survey the economy below with agony unspeakable. For the rest, there was little in the room but
depressing Victorian chairs in mahogany, and a piano
with a high back, such as our grandmothers played
upon.

When Ladd came back, he had a bottle in his hand. I
smiled openly when I saw that it was a pint; but he
decanted it with a fine show of generosity, and pushing
a glass to me, took up the matter which interested him
at once.

"Where did ye see my nephew?" he asked, while I
sipped the wine with satisfaction; "it'll have been in
London, perhaps?"

"I saw him—if he was your nephew—at Pangbourne
last night," said I; "he had a pretty woman with him,
and wanted to sell me two emeralds."

"That must have been the wife he married in San
Francisco," cried he, "but she has no sinecure; you
didn't hear that I paid his passage abroad last spring
after he'd robbed me of a thousand —— Well, and it
was emeralds he wanted to sell you?"

"Two of the finest I have ever seen," said I, "and
matching perfectly."

The import of the emeralds had evidently been lost
upon him until this time; but now of a sudden he realized
that he might be concerned in the business, and his
agitation was renewed. "I wonder what emeralds they
were?" he asked as if of himself; then turning to me,
he exclaimed, "Will you come up stairs with me a
minute?"

He did not wait for me to answer, but led the way up
bare stone steps to a landing off which there led two

N

long passages; and in a big and not uncomfortable bed-room he showed me three safes, one a little one, which he opened, and took therefrom a case containing seven emeralds of a size and quality apparently similar to the two I had seen at Pangbourne. But when he gave them to me to examine I saw at once that five of them were genuine and two were false.

"Well," said he, after I had looked at them long and closely, "how do you like them?"

"I like them well enough," said I; "at least, I like five of them, but the other two are glass!"

At this he cried, "Oh, my God!" and clutched the stones from me with the trembling fingers of a madman. When he had seen them for himself—being judge enough to follow me in my conclusions—he began to roar out oaths and complaints most pitifully, cursing his nephew as I have never heard a man cursed before or since. In my endeavour to calm him, I asked how it could possibly be that this fellow he feared had got access to his safe; but he poured out only an incoherent tale, begging me to send for the police, then not to leave him, then falling to prophecy, and declaring that he would be murdered before the month was out. It was altogether the most moving sight I have ever seen— pointing strongly to the conclusion that the man was mad; and, in fact, where his jewels were concerned, sanity was not his strong point.

By-and-by he got sufficient reason to tell me that he had the administration of some of his nephew's property, and that in his work he had first fallen foul of a man, headstrong, vindictive, by no means honest, and, in some moods, dangerous. Yet, even knowing his relative's character and the threats he had urged against him, he could not tell how the safe was broken, or by what means the emeralds had gone. He was not even aware that his nephew was in England; and I had been the first to bring intelligence of his coming. I asked him, naturally, if these two stones represented the whole of his loss, and at that he fell off again to his raving, but took two keys of the larger safes from a secret drawer in the smaller as I could see; and began to pour upon the faded bed-cover a wealth of treasure which might have bought a city. Here were rubies of infinite perfection, diamonds set in a hundred shapes, ropes of pearls, boxes of opals, bracelets of every known pattern, rings scarce to be numbered, aigrettes, necklaces—in short, such a stupendous show that the dark and dingy bedroom was lighted with wondrous light, a myriad rays flashing up from the bed, until the whole place seemed touched with a wand, and changed to a chamber of a thousand colours. Before the bed of jewels the old man stood chattering and moaning; now bathing, as it were, in the gems, now letting them ripple over his hands, or addressing tender endearments to them; or clutching them with nervous avidity as though he feared even my companionship.

In the midst of this strange scene, and while we were both held spellbound by the wondrous vision of wealth, a sudden exclamation drew the miser from his employment. It came from the girl who had been sent to the village, she now standing in the doorway of the bedroom, and crying, "Oh, good Lord!" as she saw the glitter of the gems. But Ladd turned upon her at the words, and grasped her by the wrists, crying out as he had cried when first he knew that he was robbed.

"You hussy," he hissed, bending her by the arms backward almost to the floor; "what do you watch me for? What do you mean by coming here? Where are

the emeralds you have stolen? Tell me, wench; do you
hear? Tell me, or I shall hurt you!"

He held her in so firm a grasp that I feared she would
suffocate, and went to pull him off; at which action he
turned to cry out against me; but the anger had played
upon him so that he fainted suddenly all across the bed,
and amongst the jewels. The girl, whom he had forced
upon the floor, now rose impudently, and said,—

"Did ye ever see the like of him?—but I'll make him
pay for it! Oh, you needn't look, he's that way often.
He'll come to in a minute; but he won't find me in the
house to-morrow—wages or no wages."

"Do what you like," I cried to her angrily, "but
don't chatter. Have you got any brandy in the house?"

"Brandy! and for him!" said she, arranging her
dress which he had torn; "is it me that should be running for it? Not if I know it; brandy, I like that!"

"Then leave the room," I exclaimed imperatively;
and with that she went off, banging the door behind her,
and I was alone with the man and his jewels. I think
it was the strangest situation I have ever known. Some
thousands of pounds' worth of gems lay scattered upon
the coverlet, upon the sheets, and even upon the carpet.
Ladd himself lay like the figure upon a tomb, white and
motionless; there was only the light of a common
paraffin lamp; and three parts of the room lay in darkness. My first thought was for the man's life, and
remembering that I had a flask in my pocket, I forced
brandy between his clenched teeth, and laid him flat
upon his back. In a few moments there was a percep-
tible, though very quick beat of his pulse, and after that,
when he had taken more of the spirit, he opened his
eyes, and endeavoured to raise himself; but I forbade
him roughly, and gathering up his gems I bundled them

in the greater safe, and turned the key upon them. He, however, watched me with glazing eyes, scarce being able, for lack of strength, to utter a word; but he motioned for me to give him the key, and this he placed under the pillow of his bed, and fell presently into a gentle sleep, which was of good omen.

I should mention that it was now full dark outside, and, as I judged, about the hour of ten. I had got the man's jewels into his safe for him, and he was sleeping; but where the bewitching little hussy was I did not know; or what was the value of the old man's fears about his nephew. It was clear to me, however, that he had been robbed, probably by the immediate agency of the girl who acted as his servant; and it was equally obvious that I had no alternative but to stay by him, even if prospect of probable business in the future had not moved me to do so. An inspection of his room by the flickering light of the lamp disclosed to me a small dressing-room leading from it, this containing a sofa; and when I had quite assured myself that my patient, as I chose to regard him, slept easily, and that his pulse was no longer intermittent nor faint, I took my boots off and lay down upon the hard horsehair antiquity which was to serve me for bed. Strange to say, in half an hour I fell into a dreamless sleep, for I was heavy with fatigue, and had walked many hours upon the Kennett's bank; but when I awoke, the room was utterly dark, and the screams of a dying man rang in my ears.

In moments of emergency one's individuality asserts itself in curious actions. I am somewhat stolid, and a poor subject for panics, and I remember on this particular occasion that my first act was to draw on my boots with deliberation, and even to turn in the tags carefully before I struck a match, and got a sight of the

scene which I remember so well though many months
have passed since its happening. When I had light, I
found Ladd standing by the door of his large safe, which
was open, but there was a deep crimson stain upon his
shirt, and he no longer had the voice to scream. In
fact, he was dying then; and presently he fell prone
with a deep gasp, and I knew that he was dead. In the
same instant a black shadow, as of a man, passed
between me and the flicker of the light; and as the
match went out the door of the chamber swung upon its
hinges, and the assassin passed from the room.

Now, Ladd had scarce fallen before I was in the dark
passage, listening with great tension of the ear for a
sound of the hiding man's footstep. But the place was
as still as the grave; and then there came upon me the
horrid thought that the fellow lurked with me about the
room's door, and presently would serve me as he had
served the other. Cold with fear at the possibility, I
struck a match, and advanced along the passage, using
half a box of lucifers in the attempt. At the corner I
came suddenly upon a cranny; and as the light died
away, two gleaming eyes shot up glances to mine, and
a man sprang out flashing a blade in the air, but rushing past me, and fleeing like the wind towards the
southern wing—the unfinished one. So swift did he go
that I saw nothing of his face, and it seemed scarce a
moment before I heard a door open, and another great
cry, followed by a splashing of water and utter silence.

This second cry took, I think, what little nerve I had
left; and while the echo of it was still in the passages
my last match went out. The place was now black
with unbroken darkness; every step that I took appeared to reach mysterious stairs and to send me stag-
gering; but at last a sudden patch of moonlight from a

"I STRUCK A MATCH AND GOT A SIGHT OF THE SCENE WHICH I
REMEMBERED SO WELL THOUGH MANY MONTHS HAVE PASSED SINCE ITS
HAPPENING."

corner encouraged me to go on, and I reached the spot
where the man had disappeared. At that point a door
creaked and banged upon its hinges, but the white light
coming through it saved me from the fate of him who
had gone before. It showed me at a glance that the
door was built in a side of the *unfinished* wall of the
wing, and that the man, who evidently had mistaken it
for the entrance to the back staircase, which I saw a
few feet further on, had crashed down fifty feet into the
moat below, carrying, as I supposed, his plunder in his
hands. Then I knew the meaning of the gurgling cry
and the horrid thud, and terror seemed to strike me to
my very marrow.

How I got out of the house I do not know to this day.
Thrice I made a circuit of winding corridors only to
find myself again before the room where Ladd's body
lay in the circle of moonlight which the window focused
upon the safe; thrice I reached doors which seemed to
give access to the yard; but led only into gloomy shuttered chambers where curious shapes of the yellow rays
came through the dusty crevices. At last, however, I
reached the frowsy kitchen, and the yard, and stood a
minute to breathe the chill night air, and to think what
was to be done; whither first to go; to whom to appeal.
The whine of a voice from the stable seemed to answer
me. I entered the roofless shanty, and there found the
dark-eyed girl sitting upon a rotting garden roller, and
quivering in every limb. She too was dressed ready
to accompany the man who then lay in the moat, I did
not doubt; but at the first sight of me she started up
with blanched face, and clinging to me she cried,—

"Take me away; oh, my God, take me away from
it!" and rather incoherently she muttered that she was
innocent, and protested it in a score of phrases. I saw

a flush of dawn-light upon her babyish face as she spoke, and it occurred to me when I was putting the horse to the dogcart that she was unmistakably pretty, and that her customary occupation was not that of a housemaid. But I only said to her,—

"Keep anything you have to say for the police. I am going to fetch them." And with that I drove off, and the last I saw of my lady showed her as she sat moaning on the straw, her hair tumbling upon her shoulders, and her face buried in her hands.

* * * * * *

The trial of this woman, and her acquittal by the jury, are well remembered in Caversham ; nor is the mystery of Jabez Ladd's jewels and their disappearance by any means an infrequent topic for alehouses. What became of the precious stones which Arthur Vernon Ladd, the old man's nephew, took from the safe on the night he murdered his uncle, one man alone knows— and that is myself. The people of the town will tell you that the moat was dragged and drained with no result. I myself saw the body of the murderer—the velvet-coated man of Pangbourne; but although, at least, a couple of thousand pounds worth of jewels were missing from the safe, there was not one of them about him, or to be found upon the *concrete* bottom of the moat into which he had dropped with the blood of Ladd fresh upon his hands. In vain the police searched the girl—her name was Rachel Peters, she said—and her boxes ; equally in vain the old house was ransacked from top to bottom. The thing was a black mystery, it was gossip not only for inns and beerhouses, but for the county. The report of it spread even to America, and to this moment it has remained unsolved.

The jewels being undiscoverable, and Ladd having

been murdered to my knowledge by his nephew, the girl, Rachel Peters, was, as I have said, discharged She returned to the old house for her boxes, and immediately disappeared from the knowledge of the county. Ten months later I saw her dancing on the stage of an opera house in Florida, and she was wearing *five of the seven emeralds* which Ladd had lost! The spectacle seemed so amazing to me that I sought her out between the acts, and found her as full of *chic* and *verve* as a Parisian *soubrette*. Nor did she disguise anything from me, telling me everything over a cigarette with a relish and a sparkle which was astounding to see.

"Yes," said she—but I give her story in plain words, for her way of telling it is not to be written down—" I had known Vernon Ladd for years. I doubt if there was a worse man in Europe ; but I was frightened of him, and I entered old Ladd's service at his wish to help him to steal the jewels. We got at the emeralds first because they were in the small safe ; but we didn't know where the keys of the other safe were, and we put two sham emeralds in the case to keep the old boy quiet while we worked. That night you came to the house Vernon Ladd was already inside, concealed behind the old man's bed ; and he watched you open the great safe and spread the jewels. The mischief of it was that Ladd woke up five minutes too soon, and caught the boy by the throat—you know what he got for that, for you saw it, and you know how Vernon mistook the door, and went down in a hurry. Well, when you'd gone for the police, I ran round to the back of the house, and what should I see but the bag of jewels stuck on a ledge just under the landing window. He'd dropped them as he fell, and there they were lying so plain that one could have seen them a mile off. I just ran up and reached them with my arm, but when I was in the stable again, and thinking of hiding them, I heard you driving up the road, and I slipped the bag in the first thing handy—it was your own fishing creel.

"No, you never found them, did you? just because they were hanging up there plain for every one to see. When the judge discharged me at the Court, I went again to the house to get my box, never thinking to see the stones; but you'd gone away without the creel, and it was the first thing I touched lying in the straw of the stable. You may be sure it didn't lie there long. I'd saved up enough money for a passage to the States, and when I got here I started as an actress, as I was before, and I sold the things one by one. These emeralds are all that's left—and if you're a brick, you'll buy them!"

This was her story. She was a clever woman, and having been discharged on the accusation of robbing the dead miser Ladd, could not be sent to her trial again. Her invitation for me to buy the emeralds was tempting. I had already purchased two from the unhappy lady of Pangbourne, who was married to the velvet-coated Vernon Ladd, and is now living in seclusion in Devonshire. The other five would have made the set of great value. Ladd had no heirs; it was altogether a nice point. I debated it.

THE PURSUIT OF THE TOPAZ

THE PURSUIT OF THE TOPAZ

I WAS struggling heroically to force my arms through the sleeves of a well-starched shirt, when the man knocked upon the door of my bedroom for the second time. I had heard him faintly five minutes before, when my head was as far in a basin as the limitations of Parisian toilet-ware would allow it to go; but now he knocked imperiously, and when I opened to him he stood hesitatingly with a foolish leer upon his face, and that which he meant for discretion upon his lips.

"Well," said I, "what the devil do you want? Can't you see I'm dressing?"

At this he looked with obvious pity for me towards the basin, but quickly recovered himself.

"Dame," said he, with a fine Gascon accent, "there is a lady waiting for monsieur in the *salon*."

"A lady!" cried I with surprise; "who is she?"

"I am but three days in Paris," replied he, "and she is a stranger to me. If monsieur prefers it, I will ask her some questions."

"You will please do nothing of the sort; did she give her name?"

"I seem to remember that she did, but it has escaped me. I shall say that you are engaged, and will see her to-morrow; monsieur leaves Paris at nine o'clock *hein?*"

He said this with another vulgar leer, but I turned

round upon him fiercely, for I had begun to brush what is left of my hair.

"You impudent poltroon!" exclaimed I; "leave the room instantly, and tell the lady that I will be with her in five minutes."

"Ah," said he, "it is like that then? Very good; I shall safeguard your interests; trust in me. May I be permitted to light the candles?"

He said this with a fine eye to the bill; but I sent him away after some display of temper, and finished my dressing quickly, wondering all the time who the woman was, and what she wanted of me. Although I have lived in Paris nigh as much as in London, I have cultivated few acquaintances there other than those arising in the path of business. The domestic side of Parisian life has never appealed to me; I am equally callous to the vaunted attractions of the dismal halls of light and twaddle with which the foreigner usually boasts acquaintance. It was, therefore, not only with profound surprise, but also with a piquant curiosity, that I fell to speculating upon the identity of my visitor, and the mission which brought her to me.

At the time of this occurrence I had been in the French capital for one week, being carried there by the announcement of the sale of the Countess Boccalini's jewels. After my usual custom, I had engaged rooms in the little Hôtel de Bard, which is almost the neighbour of the Grand Hotel, and had passed the week in the haggling and disputation which are the salt of life to a jeweller. The result was the purchase of a superb necklace of brilliants, which subsequently I sold here for nine thousand pounds, and of a quantity of smaller stones, and of chrysoprase, the gem which is now becoming exceedingly fashionable in London. But on the night of which I am writing, my

trading was done, and a ridiculous promise to go to the
Opera Ball alone kept me in Paris. How the promise
came to be given to my friend Tussal I cannot remember; but he had assured me that the ball was the event
of April, and that my education would remain imperfect
until I had gazed upon the spectacle of *calicots* and
flaneurs rioting in the great house which Garnier de-
signed and Delaunay painted. And so pressing was he,
and so largely did I trade with him, that I yielded at
last to his solicitations, and agreed to accept a seat in
his box.

By the terms of his invitation I was to meet him at
the Grand Café at midnight, and thence was to proceed
to the Opera House at half-past twelve. I had determined to dine quietly at my own hotel, and afterwards
to spend the intervening hours at the Théâtre de la
Porte St. Martin; for which purpose I dressed at a comparatively early hour; and dressing, received the stiff-
necked Gascon's message that a lady wished to see me.
Yet for what purpose she came, or who she might be, I
had not an idea; and I turned over a hundred theories
in my mind as I descended to the little reception room
of the hotel, and there found her sitting by the uncovered
table with a railway guide before her, but obviously
agitated, and as obviously pretty.

When looking back upon the extraordinary mystery
of which this childish girl was for me the centre, I have
often remembered that she was one of the few French-
women I have met who had a thoroughly English face.
Her skin was white and pink, untouched by that olive
tint which is so prevalent in Paris; her eyes were won-
drously blue; she had rich brown hair shot with golden
tresses, which gave to the whole a magnificent lustre;
she was entirely free of that restless gesture which is

o

the despair of a man of nerves. As I first saw her, she wore a captivating apology for a bonnet, which seemed to consist of a spray of jet and a hairpin; but her hands were gloved as only a Frenchwoman's hands are, and a long cloak of steel-gray cloth edged with fur, fell about her shoulders, yet permitted one to see an exquisite outline of figure beneath. Indeed, she made a perfect little picture, and her exceeding prettiness lost nothing for the rush of colour to her cheeks when I spoke to her.

"I am Bernard Sutton," said I; "if it is possible that I can be of any service to you, the privilege is mine——"

"Thank you a thousand times," said she, speaking with an accent which added to the charm of her English. "I have heard of you often from Madame Carmalovitch, whose husband owned the famous opal; you were very kind to her——"

"I was exceedingly sorry for her," I replied; "are you a relation of hers?"

"Oh, no!" she exclaimed; "I am Mademoiselle Edile Bernier, and I live with my mother at 32, Rue Boissière. You will laugh to hear why I come to you. It is about something you alone can advise me upon, and, of course, you will guess it at once."

"I won't waste your time by being ambiguous," said I, "you have come to consult me about some jewels; pray let me see them."

There was no one else in the *salon* at that time, the few people in the hotel being at dinner. The girl had, therefore, no hesitation in opening a bracelet-case, which she had carried under her cloak, and showing me a plain band of gold which served as a mount for a small circle of turquoise and an exceedingly large rose-pink topaz, which possessed all the lustre of a diamond. I saw at once that the gem was from Brazil, and was large

"SHE MADE A
PERFECT LITTLE
PICTURE."

enough and rich enough
to be worth a consider-
able sum, but I have never known
hunger for the topaz myself, and
when I had taken one look at the
bracelet I handed it back to her.

"It's exceedingly pretty," said I,
"and your stones are very good.
There is a little green at the base
of the larger turquoises, but you will
hardly match the topaz in Paris. Are you seeking to
know the value of it?"

"I would never ask that," she answered quickly; " it was a gift from my *fiancée*, Monsieur Georges Barré, whom you may know by name."

I vow it was very bewitching to watch the rosy blush which suffused her cheek when she made this confession. Yet she spoke with the ring of pride in her voice, and I replied to her encouragingly while she put her treasure beneath her cloak, as though she feared that other eyes than hers should rest even upon the case of it.

"Monsieur Barré is well known to me by name," said I, "his bust of Victor Hugo from last year's salon is at this moment the chief ornament of my library. I must now congratulate him for the second time."

At this she laughed, but the ripples died away quickly upon her face, and the look of haunting fear again troubled her eyes. I observed that she was reticent in speaking plainly to me, and did my best to help her out with it.

"You have not yet put to me," said I, "the precise question which brought you here. It concerns the bracelet, of course?"

"Ye—yes," said she; "but I am very much afraid you will laugh at me. I wanted to ask you if, in your judgment—that is, with your experience—there is any reason why I should not wear my present at the Opera Ball to-night?"

Her confusion, when thus she had unburdened herself, was overwhelming. She scarce dared to lift her eyes to mine as she spoke, and one of her hands played restlessly with the railway guide, while the other was closed firmly about her bracelet. Nor did I, who know the potency of woman's superstition in the matter of their jewels, feel the touch of a desire to draw amusement from her dilemma.

" Come," said I, with all the gentleness of voice I could command; " you have been reading something silly. The topaz is the emblem of fidelity, it is also a traditional cure for indigestion. In other words, the ancients were wise enough to know that love and good cooking are not so far apart after all. Wear your jewel at the opera by all means, and regard it as an antidote to the *confetti* you will consume."

She heard me thus far with a restrained smile upon her face, and indeed, she half rose as though to end the interview ; but the evidence of fear was still about her eyes, and there was the note of unsatisfied questioning in her voice when she said,—

" I was sure you would tell me that—but I am keeping you from your dinner, and have already troubled you too much I fear."

My answer to this appeal was to close the door of the *salon*, which had been open during our interview, and to draw a chair close to hers.

" Mademoiselle Bernier," said I, " the most important part of the intelligence you meant to bring to me remains unspoken. Let me encourage you to tell me everything freely, and be assured that without your express permission nothing you may say will be remembered by me."

" Thank you, very much," she said quietly, evidently regaining complete confidence; " but I have nothing to conceal. A week ago, Monsieur Barré gave me this bracelet with the stipulation that I should wear it at the ball to-night. Two days ago, I received this letter, which I hesitated to show even to you, lest it should be an injustice to the man I love."

She passed, with her words, a dirty scrap of a note to me, the leaf of a sheet of the commonest lined scribbling paper; and I read upon it, written in very bad French, the warning—

"Mademoiselle. If you wear the topaz bracelet at the Opera Ball to-night you carry death upon your arm."

Thrice I read this; and as I repeated the words, the third time aloud, I saw, shaping about the simplicity of the girl, a mystery which seemed as deep, and at first sight as unfathomable, as any as I had known. As for the momentary victim of it she sat watching me while I, all amazed, held the paper still in my hand, and did not hide my surprise, or, indeed, attempt to.

"Mademoiselle," said I, "you speak to me of very deep matters, I fear. But, of course, you have shown this letter to your relatives?"

"I have but one relative in the world," said she, "my mother, who is a paralytic. I dare not mention such a thing to her; she would die of fear."

"And you yourself have no suspicion, no faint idea of the cause of such a letter as that?"

"I cannot even attempt to guess at it."

"There are none of your lady friends who would hazard a joke with you?"

"Oh, no; they could not think of such a joke as that, and my few friends love me, I believe."

I had now begun to pace up and down the room, being in a very whirl of theory and conjecture. And, in truth, the problem presented so many possibilities that it might well have troubled a man whose whole occupation was the solution of mysteries. Not that I lacked any clue, for my knowledge, such as it is, of the heartburnings, the jealousies, and the crimes which hover over the possession of precious stones at once compelled me to the conclusion, either that M. Georges Barré had been the victim of a previous *affaire du cœur*, or that his *fiancée* had been won only over trampled hopes and vain rivalries. In either case (the case of the woman who resented the man's marriage, or the man who resented the woman's) was there ample warranty for such a letter as Mademoiselle Bernier had received. Yet was I too slow to venture the question with her, and did so at last in sheer pity for her childishness.

"Tell me," said I, stopping of a sudden before her, "what led you to me?"

"Madame Carmalovitch," said she. "I went to her first, but she knew you were in Paris, and would not rest until I had consented to see you. She would have come with me, but is latterly almost always unable to face the night air."

"You have no one else you would care to consult in such a case?"

"No one," said she.

"And if you go to the ball to-night without your bracelet——?"

She looked up at me with tears in her eyes when she answered,—

"Georges would never forgive me."

"Could you make no excuse to remain at home?"

"Oh, don't ask me to do that," she exclaimed pitifully, "I have lived for the ball since the beginning of the year!"

It was a woman's plea, and not to be resisted. I saw at once that she *would* go to the dance whatever words fell from me, and I turned from the subject to one more important.

"Since you are determined to be there to night," said I, "perhaps you will give me Monsieur Georges Barré's address?"

"Oh, for the love of God, don't tell him!" she cried;

" he would never forgive me if I distrusted his present."

" My dear lady, I quite understand that. Really, you credit me with being a very poor diplomatist. When I see him I doubt if I shall even mention your name to him."

" You promise me that ? "

" I promise you, at least, that he shall never know of your coming to me. But I must exact another promise from you—it is that you will not wear the topaz until you have my permission."

" But Georges expects me to wear it at the ball."

" He would not expect you to risk your life. And there is no reason, so far as I can see, why I should not be able to give you permission, or to refuse it, by eleven o'clock. You do not go to the opera until midnight, I presume ? "

" Monsieur Barré has promised to call in the Rue Boissière at a quarter past twelve. He has an *appartement* in the Hôtel Scribe. I can scarce go with him and leave his gift at home."

" Of course you can't, but I would suggest that, unless you hear from me by midnight, you carry it beneath your cloak as you do now. I shall meet you in the Opera House, at any rate. Meanwhile, I have one more question to put to you, forgive it from a man who is nearly old enough to be your father. Before you became the *fiancée* of Monsieur Barré was there—well, was there any other in your thoughts ? "

She looked at me with frankness shining clearly from her eyes, when she said,—

" Never for a moment. I was in a convent until last year, and I have not spoken to six men since I left,"

"That is all I want to know. We will both dine now; but first let me look at your bracelet once more."

She handed me the case again; and I, leaving her for a moment to fetch my glass, put the jewel under the strong light of the chandelier, and examined every inch of it within and without. I discovered then that which had escaped me upon first acquaintance with it. In one of the crevices of the clasp there was a blood-stain, unmistakable, even fresh, yet so concealed by the embossment of the jewels that I did not wonder she had remained in ignorance of it. But when I gave it to her again I doubt not that I was very serious, and this she observed, and made comment upon.

'You see something now which you did not see ten minutes ago," she cried; "you will surely tell me?"

"I see a very pretty pink topaz," said I, forcing a smile, "and a young lady who is missing her dinner. Come, have some confidence in me, and put all these thoughts out of your mind until I ask you to remember them again."

"I will," said she, "and can never thank you enough; you do not know what a trouble you have taken from my mind."

Here was the end of our interview, for we had come to the door of the courtyard as we spoke, and I put her at once into the neat little brougham which was waiting for her. There were but two other men, the concierge, and a short, exceedingly dark man in evening dress, about the place at that time; and as the brougham drove away it occurred to me that the latter fellow was watching me rather closely, upon which I had a good look at him; but he turned away sharply to the coffee-room, while I went to my dinner in as fine a state of bewilderment as I have known. Never in my long

years of work had I come across such a case, or one to
which a clue, save on the hypothesis of jealousy, was
so completely wanting. Yet if jealousy were the motive
of the warning, how, I asked, came the blood-stain upon
the bracelet? And if the gem had any connection with
a previous affair of Barré's, why did he give it to his
fiancée? The latter supposition seemed, in itself, sufficient to upset the whole suggestion; nor could I find
another; but I determined to call upon the sculptor at
once, and to use every device at my command in the
interests of the helpless girl who had called upon me.

It was now near to ten o'clock, and, having dined
hastily, I passed through the courtyard on my way to
the Hôtel Scribe. There I saw, to my surprise, that the
ill-visaged Italian—for so I judged he was—still loitered
about the place; but again appeared to avoid scrutiny.
This second appearance of his seemed to me—I knew
not why—as the shaping of a story from the air; but
I had no courage then to speak to him, and I walked on
down the boulevard, perceiving as I went that flam-
beaus already lighted the great Opera House, and that
the *canaille* were preparing for the riot. When at last
I came to the hotel, and sent up my card, the answer
was that Monsieur Barré had just left, and was not
expected to return until the next morning.

How completely this answer undid my purpose I
could never set down. The man was my only possible
hope. In the haste of my conclusions I had never found
time to remember that I might not catch him; that
every *flaneur* was hither and thither like a will-o'-the-
wisp on such a night. In vain I asked, nay, implored,
for information—they could give me none; and when
further importunity was plainly a farce, I had no
alternative but to go to the Rue Boissière, in the ulti-

mate hope that Barré's destination was there, and that he had called upon his *fiancée* before the hour of the appointment. But upon this I was determined, that until I had found him Mademoiselle Bernier should not wear the bracelet, though I stood at her side from that hour to midnight.

My first attempt culminating unfruitfully, I quitted the passage of the hotel, being still bent upon the journey to the Rue Boissière, and was again upon the pavement before the café, when I saw the Italian for the third time. He stood upon the very edge of the kerbstone, undisguisedly waiting for me, so that upon a sudden impulse, which had wisdom in it, I walked over to him, and this time he did not turn away.

"Forgive the question," said I, in my miserable French, "but you are betraying an interest in my movements which is unusual; in fact, you have followed me from my hotel, I think?"

"Exactly," he replied, having even less of the tongue than I had, though I make no attempt to reproduce the vagaries of his idiom. "I followed you here, as you say——"

"For what purpose, may I ask?"

"To warn you!"

"To warn me!"

"Certainly, since you carry in your pocket the topaz bracelet."

"Oh," said I, taken aback at his false conclusion, "it is that, is it? I am much obliged to you, but I don't happen to possess such a thing."

"*Mon Dieu!*" said he; "then she did not sell it to you?"

"She certainly did not!"

"And she will wear it at the ball to-night?"

"Of course!"

"Mother of God! she is a dead woman then."

It is often possible to tell from the chord of voice a man strikes in conversation whether he be friend or enemy. I knew from the sympathetic note in this earnest exclamation that I had to do with one who wished well to Mademoiselle Bernier; but the very sorrow of the words struck me chill with fear. It was plain that I must shape a bold course if I would learn the whole moment of the mystery, and observing that the stranger was a man of much shabbiness and undoubted poverty —if that might be judged by his dress—I played the only possible card at once.

"Look here," said I, "this is no time for words like this. Come into the café with me, and I will pay you fifty pounds for what you know. It shall be worth a hundred if you convince me that you have done a substantial kindness to Mademoiselle Bernier."

He looked at his watch before he made answer. Then he said,—

"The offer is a fair one, but I do not seek your money. We have two hours in which to save her, but before I go with you, you shall swear to me that anything I may tell you will never be used against me here or in any other country."

"Of course," said I; "you don't think I am a policeman, do you? I have no other interest but that of the lady."

"Nor I," said he; and he followed me into the café, but the place was so intolerably full that I bade him come with me to a little wine-shop in the Rue Lafayette, and there we found a vacant table, and I ordered his absinthe and a glass of coffee for myself. Scarcely, however, had he lighted his cigarette before he began to talk of the matter we had come upon.

"First," said he, "tell me, did Mademoiselle speak of a letter she had received?"

" I BADE HIM COME WITH ME TO A LITTLE WINE-SHOP IN THE RUE LAFAYETTE."

"She not only spoke of it, but she gave it to me to read," I replied.

"Well," said he, "I wrote it."

"I gathered that from your words," said I next; "and of course you wrote it for very good reasons?"

"You shall hear them," said he, sipping freely of his drink. "That bracelet was last worn at the *Mi-Carême* Ball in Marseilles by a girl named Berthe Duval. She was carried from the ball-room, stabbed horribly, at one o'clock in the morning. She died in my arms, for in one week she was to have been my wife."

"And the assassin?" I asked.

"Was hunted for by the police in vain," he continued. "I myself offered every shilling that I had to find him, but, despite the activity of us all, he was never so much as named. Let us go back another year—it is painful enough for me because such a retrogression recalls to me the one passion of my life—a passion beside which the affair at Marseilles is not to be spoken of. God knows that the memory of the woman I refer to is at this moment eating out my heart. She was an Italian girl, sixteen years old when she died, and I think—why should I not?—that the world has never held a more beautiful creature. Well, she wore the bracelet, now about twenty-six months ago, at the *Mardi Gras* Ball in Savona, and she fell dead before my very eyes ten minutes after she had entered the ball-room. She had drunk of poisoned coffee, and no man but one knew by whose hand the death had come to her."

"You say no man but one; that one was ——"

"Myself!"

"Then you knew who killed the other victim at Marseilles?"

"I knew, as you say; but to know and to arrest are different things."

"Have you any idea as to the man's whereabouts now?"

"Every idea; he was in Paris three days ago—he was in Paris to-day. I should judge it more than likely that he will be at the Opera Ball to-night."

Before he could say more I rose from my chair and summoned the head waiter of the place to me. Then I wrote an urgent message upon a leaf of my note-book, and despatched it by a cab to 32, Rue Boissière. The message implored Mademoiselle Bernier, as she valued her life, to leave the bracelet at home for this night at any rate.

" Now," said I, " we can talk still at our leisure. You have taken me back to Marseilles fourteen months ago ; let us have the chapter in your life which precedes that one."

He finished off his absinthe, and called for another glass before he would answer me. At last he said,—

" You ask me to speak of things which I would well forget. I have sufficent confidence in you, however to trust my safety in your hands. The story is not a long one. Three years ago I was a struggling painter in Savona, giving half my life to a study of the pictures in the cathedral—you may know the work of Antonio Semini there—and the other half to the worship of Pauline di Chigi, the daughter of a silversmith who lives over against the Hôtel Royal. Needless to tell you of my poverty, or of my belief in myself. I lived then in the day-dreams which come at the seed-time of art ; they were broken only by the waywardness of the girl, by her womanly fickleness, by the riches of the men who sought her. It would weary you to hear of my long nights of agony following the momentary success of this man or that who wooed her, of my curses upon my own poverty, of my bitterness, and sometimes even of my hopelessness. There is something of this

sort in the life of every poor man, but the romance will
scarce bear the light of others eyes; it has a place in
my story only in so far as it prompted me to steal the
topaz, if stealing is the word for the act which gave me
its possession.

"But *arrivons!* In the end of the January of last
year, I, struggling to embrace a career in which I have
failed because I have genius and no talent, obtained a
commission from the Dominican monks to go to the
Valley of San Bernardo, and to take up my residence
there while I re-touched some of the more modern and
more faded pictures in the sanctuary of Nostra Signora
di Misericordia. The shrine and village lie in the
mountains five miles above Savona. The former is now
regaining its splendour, though grievously pillaged by
the French and by later vandals. The work would have
been recreation to me had it not been for Pauline, whom
I left to the persecution of a fat and soulless trader, and
to the solicitations of her father that she would marry
him. The new lover loaded her with presents and with
the follies of speech which a middle-aged man who is
amorous can be guilty of. I could give her nothing but
the promise of a future, and that being without market
value did not convince her. While she would make
pretence of affection for me when we were alone, she
did nothing to repulse the other. Thus I left Savona
with her kisses on my lips, and rage of her wantonness
in my heart; and for three weeks I laboured patiently
in the mountain village; and my art lifted me even
beyond the spell of the girl.

"It was at the end of the third week that my thoughts
were ardently recalled to her by a circumstance which
cannot fail to appear remarkable to you. I was walking
in the late afternoon of the Sunday in the path which

leads one high amongst the mountains, here rising green and purple, and afar with snowcaps above this lovely spot; and, chancing to turn aside from the road and to plunge into a shrubbery, I sat at last upon the log of a tree perched at the side of as wild a glen as I have seen in Italy. Below me were rocks of marble—black, yellow, red—all colours; aloe trees flourished abundantly, springing from every cranny of the dell; and though the reign of winter was not done, flowers blossomed everywhere, and multitudinous shrubs were rich in green and buds. Here I sat for an hour buried in my musings, and when at last I left it was by an overgrown path across the dingle. I found then that the opposite side of the place was vastly steeper than the one by which I had descended; in fact, I mounted it with difficulty; and when near to the summit, I clung to the saplings and the branches for sheer foothold. This action brought all my trouble, for of a sudden, just as I had come to the top, a shrub to which I was holding gave at the roots, and giving, sent me rolling to the bottom again with a great quantity of soft earth all about me and my bones aching indescribably.

"For some minutes I sat, being dizzy and shaken, on the soft grass. When I could look around me I saw a strange thing. In a mound of the mould which had fallen there was a crucifix of gold. Thickly covered with the clammy earth as it was, dulled and tarnished with long burial, the value of the thing was unmistakable. Rubies were set in the hands for blood, there was a crown of diamonds for thorns; the whole was ornamented with a sprinkling of jewels, whose fire was brilliant even through the pasty clay which clung upon the cross. I need scarce tell you that all the curiosity which is a part of me was whetted at this unexpected

P

"WHEN I COULD LOOK AROUND ME I SAW A STRANGE THING."

sight; and believing that I had come upon a very mine of treasure, I shook the mould off me, and went quickly by the easier path to the hill-top and the place of the landslip.

"Twilight was now rushing through the mountains, and a steely light, soon to turn to darkness, fell upon the ravine; yet I was able still to see clearly enough for my purpose—and for my disappointment. It is true that the slip of the earth from the hill-side disclosed a cavernous hole which had been dug, no doubt, many years ago; but of the kind of treasure whose image had leaped into my mind I saw little. The few bright things that lay about in the part of the trough which remained were entirely such vessels as serve priests in the Mass. There was a pyx in silver, a paten in gold, and two smaller ones; a monstrance with some exceedingly fine diamonds and the topaz in it, and a gold chalice much indented. I judged at once that these things had been buried either when the French plunderers came to Italy, or after the trouble of '70. It was equally clear that they were the property of the Dominicans whose house was hard by; and either that their present hiding-place was unknown, or that they had been left in concealment for some reason of diplomacy. In any case, the value of the stones in the monstrance was unquestionable; but I am an Italian, as you see, and I believed then, as now, in nothing but omens. For a long while no thought of touching these things, scarce even of handling them—so strong in human flesh is the grain of early superstition—came to me. I sat there gazing at them and watching the light of the topaz sparkling even above the radiance of the smaller diamonds—sat, in fact, until it was quite dark and the miasma rose from the valley. Then, in one of those flashes of thought which often

mean much to a man, I had it in my mind that both the
diamonds and the topaz above them would sit well upon
the arms of Pauline; I even saw her in my fancy
coquetting to me for the present. I began to laugh aloud
at the other thoughts, to call them echoes of childish
schooling, to handle the chalice and the ring of jewels,
and to tell myself that there would be no bigger fool in
Europe if I did not take them. Need I tell you that the
reasoning convinced me? and quickly, as the cold of the
mist grew more intense, I took the baubles in my hand,
still lacking the courage to secure the chalice and the
crucifix, and rose to leave the place.

"Now, for the first time, I think, you are beginning to
see the point of my story. The strangest part of it yet
remains. I have told you that dark had fallen upon the
ravine as I rose up to quit it, and that mists rose thick
from the valley with the early night. You will, therefore,
easily understand my discomfiture when, reflected upon
the white curtain of fog, I saw the dancing light of a
lantern. In the next moment a man, young but ragged,
with a full-bearded face, and the cape of a priest about
his shoulders, stood swinging his lantern before me, and
looking down at the tomb of the jewels by our feet. I
know not why, but there was something of such power
and command writ upon the monk's face that I have
never called him by any other name than 'the Christ.'
With what feelings he inspired me I cannot tell you.
Terror, human terror, is no word for my experience;
my whole being seemed stricken with an apprehension
which tortured me and made my brain burn. God! the
memory shakes me even now, and I have seen him thrice
since, and the fear is greater every time I look upon his
face.

"Thus I stood facing the man when he opened his lips

to curse me. I believe now, and shall always believe, that he is nothing but a madman, whose brain has failed from long fasting. Be that as it may, his words ring yet in my ears. If you search the world through, read the curse upon Barbarossa, and all the volumes of anathema, you will never find such a blasting accusation as the man spoke when he saw the monstrance in my hand. So dreadful was it that I reeled before him; and, losing all command, I struck him down with my stick and fled the plàce. The next day I quitted the valley of San Bernardo, and in a week Pauline was wearing the topaz, set by her father as a bracelet, and the diamonds sparkled upon her fingers. She covered me with kisses for the gift, and in her embraces I forgot the madman of the hills, and my melancholy passed.

"The rest of my story you know. Pauline wore the topaz at the *Mardi Gras* Ball, and died ten minutes after she had entered the room. A year later, having fled from Italy, I became engaged *pour passer le temps* to Berthe Duval, at Marseilles. A man has many love affairs, but only one passion. I was not in love with her, but she was rich, and troubled herself to get a smattering of art-talk, which amused me. One day she found the topaz in my studio and begged it of me. She died as you have heard; and I, poor as always, and now pursued by the damning curse, came to Paris, selling the topaz on my way here to M. Georges Barré. I have never ceased to regret that which I did; I have lamented it the most since I saw the exquisite creature who is to be his wife. And when, three days ago, I discovered the madman who had cursed me at San Bernardo in the very Rue Boissière where Mademoiselle Bernier lives, I determined to save her though the deed cost me a confession and my liberty."

.   *   *   .:   *   *   *

He had ceased to speak, and had drunk off the remainder of his absinthe, while his amazing story, which I could in no way believe, went whirling through my brain, and yet gave to me no shape of reality. At the first I was led to think that he was the madman, and I cracked for sitting there and hearing the extraordinary narration he had contrived; but there was something in his manner which forbade any long continuance of the assumption; and while I had no leisure to bring critical scrutiny upon his tale, it yet impressed me to immediate action.

"Come," said I, "presuming that your picture is not highly coloured, it is quite time we were at the opera; it is striking half-past twelve now. You know what women are. Mademoiselle Bernier may wear the bracelet in the face of everything I have said; and I am inclined to think with you that it is not wise for her to do so."

"God forbid that she should," said he; and with that we went out together.

The weather at that time was cold and cheerless; a bleak wind swept round the corners of the streets; and the lights which illumined the peristyle of the great building swayed and flickered with lapping tongues of red and yellow. But once inside, the glow of light and colour passed description. Here, whirling, shouting, dancing, leaping, the maskers rioted, almost drowning with their clamour the blare of the band; the superb entrance hall was ablaze with the flash of tawdry jewels and shining raiment; kings and queens, knights and courtiers, *calicots* and clowns, swarmed up the massive staircase, struggling, screaming, pushing, regardless of everything but the madness of the scene within. It was with the greatest difficulty that I reached Tussal's

box, and therefrom looking down upon the wild carni-
val, seeing at the first but a medley of form and colour,
a reckless horde of dancers, grisettes, shepherdesses,
over whose heads *confetti* hurtled, or the *spirales*
which the youths love. What with the dust and the
scream of voices, and the chatter of the thousand
tongues, and the heroic efforts of the fiddlers, it was
almost impossible to locate anything or any one; but the
Italian, readier than I, pointed out to me at last the one
we sought; and I observed her sitting in a box quite
close to us, where she seemed to talk with all a girl's
esprit to the young sculptor at her side. A fairer
spectacle never was than that of this childish creature,
quaintly dressed in a simple gown of white and black,
with a necklace of pearls about her throat, and a bou-
quet of roses in her hand; but the very sight of her
turned me sick with fear, for she wore upon her arm
the cursed topaz, and you could see the light of it half
over the house.

The Italian and I perceived the thing at the one time;
indeed, we rose from our seats together.

"For the love of Heaven go to her!" said he; "tell the
whole story to both of them; she may not have ten
minutes to live."

He had need to say no more, for I was in the *foyer* as
he spoke; but scarce had I opened the door of Barré's
box—which was upon the ground floor, almost at the
level of the dancers—when an appalling scream rose up
even above the clamour of the throng. For one moment,
as I stood quaking with my fears, and sore tempted to
draw back, I saw nothing but a haze of white smoke, a
vision of lurid faces and black forms, and sharper than
them all, the figure of Barré himself bending over the
body of the insensible girl. Then, amidst the babbling

of voices, and the sobbing of women, and the cry of the man, which was the most bitter cry imaginable, I heard the words, " Stop the student in the black cloak—he has shot Mademoiselle ! "

But the girl lay dead, with a bullet through her heart.

*   *   *   *   *

The tragedy at the Opera House was talk for many days in Paris; but the assassin was never taken, nor indeed, heard of. The police inclined to the theory that some masquerader had discharged a pistol by accident in the heat of the riot; and to this theory most people inclined. But there was a large sympathy for M. Georges Barré, who lay near to death for many weeks after the shock, and who quitted the capital subsequently to take up his residence in London. I told him the story the Italian had narrated to me so soon as he was well enought to hear it; but, like the police of Paris who had it also, I could see that he did not believe a word of it. He sold me the topaz bracelet, however, and I have it to this day, for I want the courage to sell it.

Of the Italian I never heard again. I saw him last immediately after the drama of the ball, when he lurched away from me, wringing his hands pitifully, begging me to tell his story to the police, and crying that a curse was upon him. But I take it, in conjunction with his confession, as a little curious that a madman, described as an ecclesiastic of Savona, should have thrown himself before a train in the Gare du Nord two days after the death of Mademoiselle Bernier.

THE RIPENING RUBIES

THE RIPENING RUBIES

"THE plain fact is," said Lady Faber, "we are entertaining thieves. It positively makes me shudder to look at my own guests, and to think that some of them are criminals."

We stood together in the conservatory of her house in Portman Square, looking down upon a brilliant ball-room, upon a glow of colour, and the radiance of unnumbered gems. She had taken me aside after the fourth waltz to tell me that her famous belt of rubies had been shorn of one of its finest pendants; and she showed me beyond possibility of dispute that the loss was no accident, but another of those amazing thefts which startled London so frequently during the season of 1893. Nor was hers the only case. Though I had been in her house but an hour, complaints from other sources had reached me. The Countess of Dunholm had lost a crescent brooch of brilliants; Mrs. Kenningham-Hardy had missed a spray of pearls and turquoise; Lady Hallingham made mention of an emerald locket which was gone, as she thought, from her necklace; though, as she confessed with a truly feminine doubt, she was not positive that her maid had given it to her. And these misfortunes, being capped by the abstraction of Lady Faber's pendant, compelled me to believe that of all the startling stories of thefts which the season had

known the story of this dance would be the most remarkable.

These things and many more came to my mind as I
held the mutilated belt in my hand and examined the
fracture, while my hostess stood, with an angry flush
upon her face, waiting for my verdict. A moment's
inspection of the bauble revealed to me at once its
exceeding value, and the means whereby a pendant
of it had been snatched.

" If you will look closely," said I, " you will see that
the gold chain here has been cut with a pair of scissors.
As we don't know the name of the person who used
them, we may describe them as pickpocket's scissors."

" Which means that I am entertaining a pickpocket,"
said she, flushing again at the thought.

" Or a person in possession of a pickpocket's imple-
ments," I suggested.

" How dreadful," she cried, " not for myself, though
the rubies are very valuable, but for the others. This is
the third dance during the week at which people's
jewels have been stolen. When will it end ? "

" The end of it will come," said I, " directly that you,
and others with your power to lead, call in the police.
It is very evident by this time that some person is
socially engaged in a campaign of wholesale robbery.
While a silly delicacy forbids us to permit our guests
to be suspected or in any way watched, the person we
mention may consider himself in a terrestrial paradise,
which is very near the seventh heaven of delight. ·He
will continue to rob with impunity, and to offer up his
thanks for that generosity of conduct which refuses us
a glimpse of his hat, or even an inspection of the boots
in which he may place his plunder."

" You speak very lightly of it," she interrupted, as I

still held her belt in my hands. "Do you know that my husband values the rubies in each of those pendants at eight hundred pounds?"

"I can quite believe it," said I; "some of them are white as these are, I presume; but I want you to describe it for me, and as accurately as your memory will let you."

"How will that help to its recovery?" she asked, looking at me questioningly.

"Possibly not at all," I replied; "but it might be offered for sale at my place, and I should be glad if I had the means of restoring it to you. Stranger things have happened."

"I believe," said she sharply, "you would like to find out the thief yourself."

"I should not have the smallest objection," I exclaimed frankly; "if these robberies continue, no woman in London will wear real stones; and I shall be the loser."

"I have thought of that," said she; "but, you know, you are not to make the slightest attempt to expose any guest in my house; what you do outside is no concern of mine."

"Exactly," said I, "and for the matter of that I am likely to do very little in either case; we are working against clever heads; and if my judgment be correct, there is a whole gang to cope with. But tell me about the rubies."

"Well," said she, "the stolen pendant is in the shape of a rose. The belt, as you know, was brought by Lord Faber from Burmah. Besides the ring of rubies, which each drop has, the missing star includes four yellow stones, which the natives declare are ripening rubies. It is only a superstition, of course; but the gems are full of fire, and as brilliant as diamonds."

"I know the stones well," said I; "the Burmese will sell you rubies of all colours if you will buy them, though the blue variety is nothing more than the sapphire. And how long is it since you missed the pendant?"

"Not ten minutes ago," she answered.

"Which means that your next partner might be the thief?" I suggested. "Really, a dance is becoming a capital entertainment."

. "My next partner is my husband," said she, laughing for the first time, "and whatever you do, don't say a word to him. He would never forgive me for losing the rubies."

When she was gone, I, who had come to her dance solely in the hope that a word or a face there would cast light upon the amazing mystery of the season's thefts, went down again where the press was, and stood while the dancers were pursuing the dreary paths of a "square." There before me were the hundred types one sees in a London ball-room—types of character and of want of character, of age aping youth, and of youth aping age, of well-dressed women and ill-dressed women, of dandies and of the bored, of fresh girlhood and worn maturity. Mixed in the dazzling *mêlée*, or swaying to the rhythm of a music-hall melody, you saw the lean forms of boys; the robust forms of men; the pretty figures of the girls just out; the figures, not so pretty, of the matrons, who, for the sake of the picturesque, should long ago have been in. As the picture changed quickly, and fair faces succeeded to dark faces, and the coquetting eyes of pretty women passed by with a glance to give place to the uninteresting eyes of the dancing man, I asked myself what hope would the astutest spy have of getting a clue to the mysteries in such a room;

how could he look for a moment to name one man or one
woman who had part or lot in the astounding robberies
which were the wonder of the town? Yet I knew that
if nothing were done, the sale of jewels in London would
come to the lowest ebb the trade had known, and that I,
personally, should suffer loss to an extent which I did
not care to think about.

I have said often, in jotting down from my book a few
of the most interesting cases which have come to my
notice, that I am no detective, nor do I pretend to the
smallest gift of foresight above my fellow man. When-
ever I have busied myself about some trouble it has
been from a personal motive which drove me on, or
in the hope of serving some one who henceforth should
serve me. And never have I brought to my aid other
weapon than a certain measure of common sense. In
many instances the purest good chance has given to
me my only clue; the merest accident has set me
straight when a hundred roads lay before me. I had
come to Lady Faber's house hoping that the sight of
some stranger, a chance word, or even an impulse might
cast light upon the darkness in which we had walked
for many weeks. Yet the longer I stayed in the ball-
room the more futile did the whole thing seem. Though
I knew that a nimble-fingered gentleman might be at my
very elbow, that half-a-dozen others might be dancing
cheerfully about me in that way of life to which their
rascality had called them, I had not so much as a hand-
breadth of suspicion; saw no face that was not the face
of the dancing ass, or the smart man about town; did
not observe a single creature who led me to hazard a
question. And so profound at last was my disgust that
I elbowed my way from the ball-room in despair; and
went again to the conservatory where the palms waved

seductively, and the flying corks of the champagne
bottles made music harmonious to hear.

There were few people in this room at the moment—
old General Sharard, who was never yet known to leave
a refreshment table until the supper table was set; the
Rev. Arthur Mellbank, the curate of St. Peter's, sipping
tea; a lean youth who ate an ice with the relish of a
schoolboy; and the ubiquitous Sibyl Kavanagh, who has
been vulgarly described as a garrison hack. She was a
woman of many partialities, whom every one saw at
every dance, and then asked how she got there—a
woman with sufficient personal attraction left to remind
you that she was *passé*, and sufficient wit to make an
interval tolerable. I, as a rule, had danced once with
her, and then avoided both her programme and her
chatter; but now that I came suddenly upon her, she
cried out with a delicious pretence of artlessness, and
ostentatiously made room for me at her side.

"Do get me another cup of tea," she said; "I've been
talking for ten minutes to Colonel Harner, who has just
come from the great thirst land, and I've caught it."

"You'll ruin your nerves," said I, as I fetched her the
cup, "and you'll miss the next dance."

"I'll sit it out with you," she cried gushingly; "and
as for nerves, I haven't got any; I must have shed them
with my first teeth. But I want to talk to you—you've
heard the news, of course! Isn't it dreadful?"

She said this with a beautiful look of sadness, and for
a moment I did not know to what she referred. Then
it dawned upon my mind that she had heard of Lady
Faber's loss.

"Yes," said I, "it's the profoundest mystery I have
ever known."

"And can't you think of any explanation at all?"

she asked, as she drank her tea at a draught. "Isn't it possible to suspect some one just to pass the time?"

" 'AS FOR NERVES, I HAVEN'T GOT ANY; I MUST HAVE SHED THEM
WITH MY FIRST TEETH.' "

"If you can suggest any one," said I, "we will begin with pleasure."

Q

"Well, there's no one in this room to think of, is there?" she asked with her limpid laugh; "of course you couldn't search the curate's pockets, unless sermons were missing instead of rubies?"

"This is a case of 'sermons in stones,'" I replied, "and a very serious case. I wonder you have escaped with all those pretty brilliants on your sleeves."

"But I haven't escaped," she cried; "why, you're not up to date. Don't you know that I lost a marquise brooch at the Hayes's dance the other evening? I have never heard the last of it from my husband, who will not believe for a minute that I did not lose it in the crowd."

"And you yourself believe——"

"That it was stolen, of course. I pin my brooches too well to lose them—some one took it in the same cruel way that Lady Faber's rubies have been taken. Isn't it really awful to think that at every party we go to thieves go with us? It's enough to make one emigrate to the shires."

She fell to the flippant mood again, for nothing could keep her from that; and as there was obviously nothing to be learnt from her, I listened to her chatter sufferingly.

"But we were going to suspect people," she continued suddenly, "and we have not done it. As we can't begin with the curate, let's take the slim young man opposite. Hasn't he what Sheridan calls—but there, I mustn't say it; you know—a something disinheriting countenance?"

"He eats too many jam tarts and drinks too much lemonade to be a criminal," I replied; "besides, he is not occupied, you'll have to look in the ball-room."

"I can just see the top of the men's heads," said she, craning her neck forward in the effort. "Have you

noticed that when a man is dancing, either he stargazes
in ecstasy, as though he were in heaven, or looks down
to his boots—well, as if it were the other thing?"

"Possibly," said I; "but you're not going to con-
stitute yourself a *vehmgericht* from seeing the top of
people's heads."

"Indeed," she cried, "that shows how little you know;
there is more character in the crown of an old man's
head than is dreamt of in your philosophy, as what's-
his-name says. Look at that shining roof bobbing up
there, for instance; that is the halo of port and honesty
—and a difficulty in dancing the polka. Oh! that mine
enemy would dance the polka—especially if he were
stout."

"Do you really possess an enemy?" I asked, as she
fell into a vulgar burst of laughter at her own humour;
but she said,—

"Do I possess one? Go and discuss me with the
other women—that's what I tell all my partners to do;
and they come back and report to me. It's as good as a
play!"

"It must be," said I, "a complete extravaganza. But
your enemy has finished his exercise, and they are going
to play a waltz. Shall I take you down?"

"Yes," she cried, "and don't forget to discuss me
Oh, these crushes!"

She said this as we came to the press upon the corner
of the stairs leading to the ball-room, a corner where
she was pushed desperately against the banisters. The
vigour of the polka had sent an army of dancers to the
conservatory, and for some minutes we could neither
descend nor go back; but when the press was somewhat
relieved, and she made an effort to progress, her dress
caught in a spike of the iron-work, and the top of a

panel of silk which went down one side of it was ripped
open and left hanging. For a minute she did not notice
the mishap; but as the torn panel of silk fell away
slightly from the more substantial portion of her dress,
I observed, pinned to the inner side of it, a large crescent
brooch of diamonds. In the same instant she turned
with indescribable quickness, and made good the
damage. But her face was scarlet in the flush of its
colour; and she looked at me with questioning eyes.

"What a miserable accident," she said. "I have
spoilt my gown."

"Have you?" said I sympathetically, "I hope it was
not my clumsiness—but really there doesn't seem much
damage done. Did you tear it in front?"

There was need of very great restraint in saying this.
Though I stood simply palpitating with amazement, and
had to make some show of examining her gown, I knew
that even an ill-judged word might undo the whole good
of the amazing discovery, and deprive me of that which
appeared to be one of the most astounding stories of the
year. To put an end to the interview, I asked her
laughingly if she would not care to see one of the maids
upstairs, and she jumped at the excuse, leaving me
upon the landing to watch her hurriedly mounting to
the bedroom story above.

When she was gone, I went back to the conservatory
and drank a cup of tea, always the best promoter of
clear thought; and for some ten minutes I turned the
thing over in my mind. Who was Mrs. Sibyl Kavanagh,
and why had she sewn a brooch of brilliants to the
inside of a panel of her gown—sewn it in a place where
it was as safely hid from sight as though buried in the
Thames? A child could have given the answer—but
a child would have overlooked many things which were

vital to the development of the unavoidable conclusion
of the discovery. The brooch that I had seen corre-
sponded perfectly with the crescent of which Lady
Dunholme was robbed—yet it was a brooch which a
hundred women might have possessed ; and if I had
simply stepped down and told Lady Faber, " the thief
you are entertaining is Mrs. Sibyl Kavanagh," a slander
action with damages had trodden upon the heels of the
folly. Yet I would have given a hundred pounds to
have been allowed full inspection of the whole panel of
the woman's dress—and I would have staked an equal
sum that there had been found in it the pendant of the
ripening rubies; a pendant which seemed to me the one
certain clue that would end the series of jewel robberies,
and the colossal mystery of the year. Now, however,
the woman had gone upstairs to hide in another place
whatever she had to hide ; and for the time it was unlikely that a sudden searching of her dress would add to
my knowledge.

A second cup of tea helped me still further on my
path. It made quite clear to me the fact that the woman
was the recipient of the stolen jewels, rather than the
actual taker of them. She, clearly, could not use the
scissors which had severed Lady Faber's pendant from
the ruby belt. A skilful man had in all probability done
that—but which man, or perhaps men ? I had long felt
that the season's robberies were the work of many
hands. Chance had now marked for me one pair ; but it
was vastly more important to know the others. The
punishment of the woman would scarce stop the wide-
spread conspiracy ; the arrest of her for the possession
of a crescent brooch, hid suspiciously it is true, but a
brooch of a pattern which abounded in every jeweller's
shop from Kensington to Temple Bar, would have been

consummate lunacy. Of course, I could have taken
cab to Scotland Yard, and have told my tale; but with
no other support, how far would that have availed me?
If the history of the surpassingly strange case were
to be written, I knew that I must write it, and lose
no moment in the work.

I had now got a sufficient grip upon the whole situation to act decisively, and my first step was to re-enter
the ball-rcom, and to take a partner for the next waltz.
We had made some turns before I discovered that Mrs.
Kavanagh was again in the room, dancing with her
usual dash, and seemingly in no way moved by the
mishap. As we passed in the press, she even smiled at
me, saying, " I've set full sail again "; and her whole
bearing convinced me of· her belief that I had seen
nothing.

At the end of my dance my own partner, a pretty
little girl in pink, left me with the remark, " You're
awfully stupid to-night! I ask you if you've seen *Manon
Lescaut*, and the only thing you say is, ' The panel
buttons up, I thought so.'" This convinced me that it
was dangerous to dance again, and I waited in the room
only until the supper was ready, and Mrs. Kavanagh
passed me, making for the dining-room, on the arm of
General Sharard. I had loitered to see what jewels she
wore upon her dress; and when I had made a note of
them, I slipped from the front door of the house un-
observed, and took a hansom to my place in Bond Street.

At the second ring of the bell my watchman opened
the door to me; and while he stood staring with profound
surprise, I walked straight to one of the jewel cases in
which our cheaper jewels are kept, and took therefrom
a spray of diamonds, and hooked it to the inside of my
coat. Then I sent the man up stairs to awaken Abel,

and in five minutes my servant was with me, though he
wore only his trousers and his shirt.

"Abel," said I, "there's good news for you. I'm on
the path of the gang we're wanting."

"Good God, sir!" cried he, "you don't mean that!"

"Yes," said I, "there's a woman named Sibyl
Kavanagh in it to begin with, and she's helped herself
to a couple of diamond sprays, and a pendant of rubies
at Lady Faber's to-night. One of the sprays I know
she's got; if I could trace the pendant to her, the case
would begin to look complete."

"Whew!" he ejaculated, brightening up at the
prospect of business. "I knew there was a woman in
it all along—but this one, why, she's a regular flier,
ain't she, sir?"

"We'll find out her history presently. I'm going
straight back to Portman Square now. Follow me in a
hansom, and when you get to the house, wait inside my
brougham until I come. But before you do that, run
round to Marlborough Street police-station and ask them
if we can have ten or a dozen men ready to mark a
house in Bayswater some time between this and six
o'clock to-morrow morning."

"You're going to follow her home then?"

"Exactly, and if my wits can find a way I'm going to
be her guest for ten minutes after she quits Lady
Faber's. They're sure to let you have the men either at
Marlborough Street or at the Harrow Road station.
This business has been a disgrace to them quite long
enough."

"That's so, sir; King told me yesterday that he'd
bury his head in the sand if something didn't turn up
soon. You haven't given me the exact address though."

"Because I haven't got it. I only know that the

woman lives somewhere near St. Stephen's Church—
she sits under, or on, one of the curates there. If you
can get her address from her coachman, do so. But go
and dress and be in Portman Square at the earliest
possible moment."

It was now very near one o'clock, indeed the hour
struck as I passed the chapel in Orchard Street; and
when I came into the square I found my own coachman
waiting with the brougham at the corner by Baker
Street. I told him, before I entered the house, to expect
Abel; and not by any chance to draw up at Lady
Faber's. Then I made my way quietly to the ball-room
and observed Mrs. Kavanagh—I will not say dancing,
but hurling herself through the last figure of the
lancers. It was evident that she did not intend to quit
yet awhile; and I left her to get some supper, choosing
a seat near to the door of the dining-room, so that any
one passing must be seen by me. To my surprise, I had
not been in the room ten minutes when she suddenly
appeared in the hall, unattended, and her cloak wrapped
round her; but she passed without perceiving me; and
I, waiting until I heard the hall door close, went out
instantly and got my wraps. Many of the guests had
left already, but a few carriages and cabs were in the
square, and a linkman seemed busy in the distribution
of unlimited potations. It occurred to me that if Abel
had not got the woman's address, this man might give it
to me, and I put the plain question to him.

"That lady who just left," said I, "did she have a
carriage or a cab?"

"Oh, you mean Mrs. Kevenner," he answered thickly,
"she's a keb, she is, allus takes a hansom, sir; 192,
Westbourne Park I don't want to ask when I see
her, sir."

Thank you," said I, "she has dropped a piece of jewellery in the hall, and I thought I would drive round and return it to her."

He looked surprised, at the notion, perhaps, of any one returning anything found in a London ball-room; but I left him with his astonishment and entered my carriage. There I found Abel crouching down under the front seat, and he met me with a piteous plea that the woman had no coachman, and that he had failed to obtain her address.

"Never mind that," said I, as we drove off sharply, "what did they say at the station?"

"They wanted to bring a force of police round, and arrest every one in the house, sir. I had trouble enough to hold them in, I'm sure. But I said that we'd sit down and watch if they made any fuss, and then they gave in. It's agreed now that a dozen men will be at the Harrow Road station at your call till morning. They've a wonderful confidence in you, sir."

"It's a pity they haven't more confidence in themselves—but, anyway, we are in luck. The woman's address is 192, Westbourne Park, and I seem to remember that it is a square."

"I'm sure of it," said he; "it's a round square in the shape of an oblong, and one hundred and ninety two is at the side near Durham something or other; we can watch it easily from the palings."

After this, ten minutes' drive brought us to the place, and I found it as he had said, the "square" being really a triangle. Number one hundred and ninety-two was a big house, its outer points gone much to decay, but lighted on its second and third floors; though so far as I could see, for the blinds of the drawing-room were up, no one was moving. This did not deter me, however and, taking my stand with Abel at the corner where two great trees gave us perfect shelter, we waited silently for many minutes, to the astonishment of the constable upon the beat, with whom I soon settled ; and to his satisfaction.

"Ah," said he, "I knew they was rum 'uns all along ; they owe fourteen pounds for milk, and their butcher ain't paid ; young men going in all night, too—why, there's one of them there now."

I looked through the trees at his words, and saw that he was right. A youth in an opera hat and a black coat was upon the doorstep of the house ; and as the light of a street lamp fell upon his face, I recognised him. He was the boy who had eaten of the jam-tarts so plentifully at Lady Faber's—the youth with whom Sibyl Kavanagh had pretended to have no acquaintance when she talked to me in the conservatory. And at the sight of him, I knew that the moment had come.

"Abel," I said, "it's time you went. Tell the men to bring a short ladder with them. They'll have to come in by the balcony—but only when I make a sign. The signal will be the cracking of the glass of that lamp you can see upon the table there. Did you bring my pistol ? "

"Would I forget that ? " he asked; "I brought you two, and look out ! for you may want them."

"I know that," said I, "but I depend upon you. Get back at the earliest possible moment, and don't act until I give the signal. It will mean that the clue is complete."

He nodded his head, and disappeared quickly in the direction where the carriage was; but I went straight up to the house, and knocked loudly upon the door. To my surprise, it was opened at once by a thick-set man in livery, who did not appear at all astonished to see me.

"They're upstairs, sir, will you go up?" said he.

"Certainly," said I, taking him at his word. "Lead the way."

This request made him hesitate.

"I beg your pardon," said he, "I think I have made a mistake—I'll speak to Mrs. Kavanagh."

Before I could answer he had run up the stairs nimbly; but I was quick after him; and when I came upon the landing, I could see into the front drawing-room, where there sat the woman herself, a small and oldish man with long black whiskers, and the youth who had just come into the room. But the back room, which gave off from the other with folding-doors, was empty; and there was no light in it. All this I perceived in a momentary glance, for no sooner had the serving-man spoken to the woman, than she pushed the youth out upon the balcony, and came hurriedly to the landing, closing the door behind her.

"Why, Mr. Sutton," she cried, when she saw me, "this is a surprise; I was just going to bed."

"I was afraid you would have been already gone," said I with the simplest smile possible, "but I found a diamond spray in Lady Faber's hall just after you had left. The footman said it must be yours, and as I am going out of town to-morrow, I thought I would risk leaving it to-night."

I handed to her as I spoke the spray of diamonds I had taken from my own show-case in Bond Street; but while she examined it she shot up at me a quick searching glance from her bright eyes, and her thick sensual lips were closed hard upon each other. Yet, in the next instant, she laughed again, and handed me back the jewel.

"I'm indeed very grateful to you," she exclaimed,

"but I've just put my spray in it's case; you want to give me some one else's property."

"Then it isn't yours?" said I, affecting disappointment. "I'm really very sorry for having troubled you."

"It is I that should be sorry for having brought you here," she cried. "Won't you have a brandy and seltzer or something before you go?"

"Nothing whatever, thanks," said I. "Let me apologise again for having disturbed you—and wish you 'Good-night.'"

She held out her hand to me, seemingly much reassured; and as I began to descend the stairs, she re-entered the drawing-room for the purpose, I did not doubt, of getting the man off the balcony. The substantial lackey was then waiting in the hall to open the door for me; but I went down very slowly, for in truth the whole of my plan appeared to have failed; and at that moment I was without the veriest rag of an idea. My object in coming to the house had been to trace, and if possible to lay hands upon the woman's associates, taking her, as I hoped, somewhat by surprise; yet though I had made my chain more complete, vital links were missing; and I stood no nearer to the forging of them. That which I had to ask myself, and to answer in the space of ten seconds, was the question, "Now, or to-morrow?"— whether I should leave the house without effort, and wait until the gang betrayed itself again; or make some bold stroke which would end the matter there and then. The latter course was the one I chose. The morrow, said I, may find these people in Paris or in Belgium; there never may be such a clue again as that of the ruby pendant—there never may be a similar opportunity of taking at least three of those for whom we had so long hunted. And with this thought a whole plan of action suddenly

"'I—I WON'T SPEAK, SIR,' HE GASPED."

leaped up in my mind; and I acted upon it, silently and swiftly, and with a readiness which to this day I wonder at.

I now stood at the hall-door, which the lackey held open. One searching look at the man convinced me that my design was a sound one. He was obtuse, patronising, —but probably honest. As we faced each other I suddenly took the door-handle from him, and banged the door loudly, remaining in the hall. Then I clapped my pistol to his head (though for this offence I surmise that a judge might have given me a month), and I whispered fiercely to him:—

"This house is surrounded by police; if you say a word I'll give you seven years as an accomplice of the woman upstairs, whom we are going to arrest. When she calls out, answer that I'm gone, and then come back to me for instructions. If you do as I tell you, you shall not be charged—otherwise, you go to jail."

At this speech the poor wretch paled before me, and shook so that I could feel the tremor all down the arm of his which I held.

"I—I won't speak, sir," he gasped. "I won't, I do assure you—to think as I should have served such folk."

"Then hide me, and be quick about it—in this room here, it seems dark. Now run upstairs and say I'm gone."

I had stepped into a little breakfast-room at the back of the dining-room, and there had gone unhesitatingly under a round table. The place was absolutely dark, and was a vantage ground, since I could see therefrom the whole of the staircase; but before the footman could mount the stairs, the woman came half-way down them, and, looking over the hall, she asked him,—

" Is that gentleman gone ? "

" Just left, mum," he replied.

" Then go to bed, and never let me see you admit a stranger like that again."

She went up again at this, and he turned to me, asking,—

"What shall I do now, sir ? I'll do anything if you'll speak for me, sir ; I've got twenty years' kerecter from Lord Walley ; to think as she's a bad 'un—it's hardly creditable."

"I shall speak for you," said I, " if you do exactly what I tell you. Are any more men expected now ? "

" Yes, there's two more ; the capting and the clergymin, pretty clergymin he must be, too."

"Never mind that ; wait and let them in. Then go upstairs and turn the light out on the staircase as if by accident. After that you can go to bed."

" Did you say the police was 'ere ? " he asked in his hoarse whisper ; and I said,—

" Yes, they're everywhere, on the roof, and in the street, and on the balcony. If there's the least resistance, the house will swarm with them."

What he would have said to this I cannot tell, for at that moment there was another knock upon the front door, and he opened it instantly. Two men, one in clerical dress, and one, a very powerful man, in a Newmarket coat, went quickly upstairs, and the butler followed them. A moment later the gas went out on the stairs ; and there was no sound but the echo of the talk in the front drawing-room.

The critical moment in my night's work had now come. Taking off my boots, and putting my revolver at the half-cock, I crawled up the stairs with the step of a cat, and entered the back drawing-room. One of the folding doors of this was ajar, so that a false step would probably have cost me my life—and I could not possibly tell if the police were really in the street, or only upon their way. But it was my good luck that the men talked loudly, and seemed actually to be disputing. The first thing I observed on looking through the open door was that the woman had left the four to themselves. Three of them stood about the table whereon the lamp was; the dumpy man with the black whiskers sat in his arm-chair. But the most pleasing sight of all was that of a large piece of cotton-wool spread upon the table and almost covered with brooches, lockets, and sprays of diamonds; and to my infinite satisfaction I saw Lady Faber's pendant of rubies lying conspicuous even amongst the wealth of jewels which the light showed.

There then was the clue; but how was it to be used? It came to me suddenly that four consummate rogues such as these were would not be unarmed. Did I step into the room, they might shoot me at the first sound; and if the police had not come, that would be the end of it. Had opportunity been permitted to me, I would, undoubtedly, have waited five or ten minutes to assure myself that Abel was in the street without. But this was not to be. Even as I debated the point, a candle's light shone upon the staircase; and in another moment Mrs. Kavanagh herself stood in the doorway watching me. For one instant she stood, but it served my purpose; and as a scream rose upon her lips, and I felt my heart thudding against my ribs, I threw open the folding doors, and deliberately shot down the glass of the lamp which had cast the aureola of light upon the stolen jewels.

As the glass flew, for my reputation as a pistol shot was not belied in this critical moment, Mrs. Kavanagh

"IN ANOTHER MOMENT MRS. KAVANAGH HERSELF STOOD IN THE DOOR-
WAY WATCHING ME."

R

ran in a wild fit of hysterical screaming to her bedroom above—but the four men turned with loud cries to the door where they had seen me; and as I saw them coming, I prayed that Abel might be there. This thought need not have occurred to me. Scarce had the men taken two steps when the glass of the balcony windows was burst in with a crash, and the whole room seemed to fill with police.

*   *   *   *   *   *

I cannot now remember precisely the sentences which were passed upon the great gang (known to police history as the Westbourne Park gang) of jewel thieves; but the history of that case is curious enough to be worthy of mention. The husband of the woman Kavanagh—he of the black whiskers—was a man of the name of Whyte, formerly a manager in the house of James Thorndike, the Universal Provider near the Tottenham Court Road. Whyte's business had been to provide all things needful for dances; and, though it astonishes me to write it, he had even found dancing men for many ladies whose range of acquaintance was narrow. In the course of business, he set up for himself eventually; and as he worked, the bright idea came to him, why not find as guests men who may snap up, in the heat and the security of the dance, such unconsidered trifles as sprays, pendants, and lockets. To this end he married, and his wife being a clever woman who fell in with his idea, she—under the name of Kavanagh— made the acquaintance of a number of youths whose business it was to dance; and eventually wormed herself into many good houses. The trial brought to light the extraordinary fact that no less than twenty-three men and eight women were bound in this amazing conspiracy, and that Kavanagh acted as the buyer of the property they stole, giving them a third of the profits, and swindling them outrageously. He, I believe, is now taking the air at Portland; and the other young men are finding in the exemplary exercise of picking oakum, work for idle hands to do.

As for Mrs. Kavanagh, she was dramatic to the end of it; and, as I learnt from King, she insisted on being arrested in bed.

MY LADY OF THE SAPPHIRES

MY LADY OF THE SAPPHIRES

A PHOTOGRAPH of My Lady of the Sapphires is hung immediately opposite to the writing-table in my private office. It is there much on the principle which compels a monk to set a skull upon his praying-stool, or a son of Mohammed to ejaculate pious phrases at the call of the muezzin. "*Nemo solus sapit,*" wrote Plautus. Had Fate cast him in the mould of a jeweller, rather than that of a playwright, he would have set down a stronger phrase.

I first saw My Lady two years ago, though it was only upon the day of my introduction that I learnt her name. She had then, though I knew it not, been before the town for many weeks as a physiognomist, a mistress of the stars, a reader of faces, and in many other capacities interesting to the idle and the credulous. Society, which laughed at her predictions, paid innumerable guineas for the possession of them; great dames sat in her boudoir and discussed amatory possibilities; even the youth of the city, drawn by the prettiness of her manner and her unquestionable good looks, came cheerfully to hear that they would have money "from two sources," or had passed through the uninteresting complaints of infancy without harm. In her way, she was the event of the season. Dowagers scolded her, but came again and again to probe family secrets, and learn the hidden things about their husbands; men flocked to her to know what possibility there was of an early return to the bliss of single life; mere boys ventured upon the hazard of a little mild flirtation—and were at once shown the door by a formidable lackey. Throughout her career scandal never lifted its voice against her. She was engaged ultimately to Jack Lucas, and her marriage was as brilliant as her career had been fortunate.

When a curious chance and combination of events first brought me to acquaintance with her she was in the very height of her practice. Carriages crowded daily in Dover Street—where, with her mother, she had rooms— and it was the thing to consult her. Yet, until I dined casually one night with Colonel Oldfield, the collector of cat's-eyes, and Bracebridge, at the Bohemian Club, hard by her house, I had never heard of her. The conversation turned during the soup—when talk is always watery —upon the press of broughams in the street without, and Oldfield mentioned her history to me, and the surprising nature of many things she had told him.

"It is easy enough," said he, "to look at a man's hand and deduce scarlet-fever and measles somewhere between two and twelve years of age; but when a woman tells you calmly that you were ready to die for two other women at the age of one-and-twenty, it's a thing to make you pause."

"Which I hope you did," exclaimed Bracebridge. "Love is distinctly a matter for specialisation."

"I did pause, sir," said the Colonel severely, "and that's where her cleverness comes in. She told me that neither of the women cared the snap of a finger for me, and I have really come to the conclusion that she was right. Years put a glamour upon most things, but it is hard, even at fifty, to recall a woman's 'no' of thirty years ago."

"Memory is a dangerous vice which should be controlled," said Bracebridge; " if you want peace, you must learn to forget. There should be no yesterday for the man of the world. But I know the morbid kind of recollection you speak about. There was a fellow here only the other night who kept a proposal book. He put the ' noes ' on one side, and the ' ayes ' on the other, and balanced the columns every Christmas. One day he left the book in a cab, and has spent his time since going to Scotland Yard for it. That comes of reminiscences! "

" I agree with you in the main," said the Colonel; "there is very little in any man's private life which is of concern to any one but himself. The lady we are speaking of knows this, and makes her fortune by her knowledge. The truth is that we all love a little plain-spokenness. There is far too much praise about. Tell a fool that he is not a clever man discreetly, and you flatter him; inform him that he is a brainless ass, and he will kick you. But when you put a black cap on your head, and take a wand in your hand, and charge a guinea for the spectacle, the fool will hear of his folly cheerfully."

" Then the girl you mention is a mere vulgar fortune-teller," said I, intervening for the first time; " it's astonishing how little difference there is, when you come to reckon it up, between the tastes of a grand dame and the tastes of her cook. The one goes in at the front door to get her hand read for a guinea; the other goes out of the back to have an equally plausible delineation for six-pence. Credulity does not know any distinction of class; in the case I mention rank is represented by one pound odd. Those of us who have no particular objection to spill salt, shiver to see the new moon through glass. That man alone who tells you frankly that he believes in all superstitions is free from the blemish. But common fortune-telling, I confess, leaves me unmoved."

"If it began and ended in the mere vulgar allotment of tragedy and of marriage, I should agree with you," said Bracebridge, speaking with unusual seriousness; "but I am inclined to think that this is a case of note-worthy cleverness, or at least of uncommon wit. The girl, possibly, is a charlatan; but if one half said of her be true, she is the *best* at the profession we have known. And after all, it's an achievement to be *the* best at some occupation, if it's only that of picking pockets."

"Speaking of that," said Oldfield, "I once knew a man in the '60th' who was proud because a society paper described him as the finest idler in Europe. That was a negative distinction of surpassing beauty, you must admit. In the lady's case, however, there is something substantial to praise. She can talk of things of which I would not attempt to spell the name, with a fluency which is charming, if it is not accurate; she has a room full of unreadable books; and I believe there are a dozen men in town who will swear that she has made diamonds before their very eyes. That should interest you, Sutton. A woman who is the possessor of what she calls the 'alkahest' or universal solvent, is not to be interviewed for a guinea every day. Besides, she might give you some useful hints."

"And who knows," said Bracebridge, "what might come of it. I presume you pay three pounds odd an ounce for the genuine metal to-day. Under certain con-tingencies, you might get it for threepence, and a wife into the bargain."

I listened to their banter with amusement for some minutes, and then cut in a little seriously.

"I did not know," said I, "that physiognomy and

alchemy usually ran well in double harness, but I must take your word for it. Anything of this sort is always amusing to a jeweller, though he is apt to get a little too much of it. The last gold maker who came to me began by promising to make a million in six months, and ended by wanting to borrow half-a-crown. I've seen scores of that sort."

"You may laugh at her as much as you please," said Oldfield; "but of one thing be assured. If I am any judge of precious stones at all, she can make rubies, and good ones too. She cast one for me when I was last at her place, and I offered her fifty pounds upon the spot for it. A quack would have taken the money, but she refused it; you couldn't want any better proof of her *bona fides* than that."

"Pardon me," I interrupted, "but I can't accept the conclusion. Probably the ruby you thought she made was the only one in the place. It was like the stock knife of the Cheap Jack. You couldn't expect her to part with it."

"Certainly I did. If she had made only one stone, I should have jumped to your opinion; but she turned them out by the dozen. Most of them were small; some were altogether too insignificant to notice. One only, as I say, was substantial; and in explanation of that, she admitted her want of control over the action of the crystals in the crucible. Sometimes they will prove worth money; more often they are quite without value. But she has hopes that the day will come when she will complete a discovery which will astonish the universe."

"They all hope that," said I; "but the universe remains unmoved."

"And, of course, you don't believe a word of it," cried

Bracebridge, as he helped himself to salad. "Well, it's part of your business, I suppose, to believe only in what you see, and not altogether in that. But the Colonel's right about the girl, and I can second every word he says. She made a piece of gold as big as your thumbnail before my very eyes. There was no pretence of humbug about it; and I may tell you that she'll only do this sort of thing for those she knows well. If you went to her to-morrow, and said, 'I want to see your experiments,' she'd laugh at you, and send you away feeling like a fool."

"And seriously," said I, beginning to experience a glimmer of interest, "you believe that she has discovered something of importance?"

"Seriously I do; and if you went to her house you would swear by her for the next month, possibly for two."

"You don't convince me at all," I replied, trying to look utterly unconcerned. "I have known too many gold-makers for that. Some of them are now in work-houses; others are in prison. One of the last got three months for stealing an overcoat, which was ridiculously unromantic."

"Not at all," said the Colonel; "theft is a complex subject capable of analysis. A thief is a man who buys in the cheapest market. We all try to do that in our way. There is no earthly reason why a *savant*, who is near to possessing the philosopher's stone, should not be charged before a magistrate with stealing a red herring. Life is all contrasts, and the contrast we speak of is a very pretty one. Go and see her at your earliest opportunity."

"That's my advice too," said Bracebridge; "and if you've a fancy to watch her at the crucible, I'll speak for you. What's more, I'll bet you an even hundred pounds that you admit my conclusions."

"Which are?" I asked.

"That she has come nearer to the solution of the diamond problem than any man or woman living or dead."

"I don't bet on certainties," said I; "but if you care to trouble the lady to burn her doubtlessly pretty hands on my account, well, let's have the interview by all means. If she convinces me that she can make any sort of precious stone worth selling in the market, I'll give a hundred pounds to a children's hospital—the Colonel can name it."

"Is it a serious offer?" asked the Colonel, looking, as I thought, a little meaningly at Bracebridge, but I said,—

"I was never more serious, and town will be quite dismal enough after this week" (it was the week of Goodwood). "Fix it up as early as you can; and conjure the lady, whose name I have not yet had the pleasure of hearing, to take care of your reputations. If she can cast me a ruby or a sapphire worth looking at, I will set it in diamonds and make her a present of it. You may tell her so from me."

"I'll give her your message undiluted," said Bracebridge, with a great deal of content, "but I'll warrant that she'll have the laugh of you, and so shall we."

They said no more upon the matter until the end of the dinner; and it was not referred to in the smoking-room after. We quitted the club at an early hour to hear a song at a music-hall which the Colonel raved about; and after that I left them and returned to Bayswater, with the recollection of my rash promise gone clean out of my head. I did not even recall it on the following

morning, and it was some three days after that I received
a note from the Colonel saying that he had, during Bracebridge's absence from town, made an appointment for
me with Miss Jessie Fleming—for such was the fair
alchemist's name—and that she would be glad to tell me
anything she could about her work on the following
afternoon at half-past two o'clock. The letter at once
brought to my mind the whole of the conversation at the
club. I remembered with a smile of contempt that the
lady was to show me, during a short interview, how the
whole of a jeweller's occupation was soon to be done
with; how diamonds and sapphires, and even the
precious metal itself, were presently to be as common as
pebbles in a brook; and I concluded with easy assurance
that if any children's hospital depended upon my being
convinced, it would have to close its doors at an early
date. I had seen so much of this sort of thing; so many
stories of fortunes lying in a metal pot had been
whispered into my ear; this could be but an addition
to the list; it remained to see if it would be an amusing
addition.

I will confess readily that if the pretender had been a
man, I would have declined curtly to see him. The
whole of those who had come to me hitherto with a pretended insight into the arcana of metals were men—
mostly half-pay officers—whose wits were half gone
with their money. Here, however, was, by all accounts,
a charming professor of the lost art. The season was
beginning to be dull; there were no more " at homes ";
possibly she would amuse me. I had given my promise
to the men—and to put it briefly I found myself at Miss
Jessie Fleming's door on the following day, not a little
expectant, disdainfully incredulous, and exceedingly anxi-
ous to prove for myself if the physiognomist's personal

attractions were even a tithe of those which had been
claimed for her by so many long-headed and usually
sensible men.

My knock at the modest-looking portal was answered

"THREE WOMEN, ALL WELL KNOWN IN SOCIETY, WERE
ENGAGED IN AN HEROIC EFFORT TO APPEAR ABSORBED IN THE
ILLUSTRATED PAPERS."

by a formidable flunky, who did not wait to hear my
name, but conducted me up a staircase draped almost to
darkness with heavy curtains, and so to a well-furnished
waiting-room on the first floor. Here three women, all
well known in society, were engaged in an heroic effort

to appear absorbed in the illustrated papers; but they were obviously uncomfortable at my presence, and cast furtive looks over the pages as though in appeal to me to make no mention of anything I had seen. I had no opportunity, however, to abate their fear of publicity; for scarce was I come into the room when the flunky appeared again at the folding-doors which cut it off from the sanctum of My Lady, and beckoned me to follow him.

I had come out on this expedition purely, as I have said, to be amused. When I found myself at last before the new Pythia of London, enthroned as she was for the immediate interpretation of the oracle, I confess that I did not foresee any disappointment of the venture. The room was half in darkness, but there was light enough by which to observe many fine pieces of china and delicate sketches upon its gold and green walls; and to note the quaint conceits of the whole scheme of decoration. A lamp of Eastern shape spread a soft red glow upon sofas and seductive lounges; a conservatory, heaped up with shade-suggesting palms, gave off at one end of it through doors of exquisitely coloured glass; there was a strange tripod of brass before the fireplace; and flowers everywhere, seeming to grow from the very grate, to flourish in all the crannies, to cover tables and bookcases, and even to decorate the dress of the young girl who now stood to receive me, and welcomed me with cordiality.

My first impression of the physiognomist—an impression which remains with me—was the outcome of her extremely youthful appearance. I am certain that whatever age she might have been she did not look it. Youth in rich generosity was stamped upon her slightest action and her most serious word. It flashed from her eyes, was seen in the unsurpassable freshness of her complexion, in the golden sheen of her hair, in the rotundity of her arms, and the development of her slight but well-formed figure. If she had any serious mood, it was not apparent when first I spoke to her; nor did a rapid analysis of her face tell me of any uncommon mental power. Her chin was a firm one, it is true; but I noticed that she had little height of head above her ears, and that there was even something of weakness in her forehead. At the same time there could not be two opinions of the general charm of her manner; and she possessed in a very large degree that magnetic power of attracting sympathy and admiration which is peculiarly the attribute of women.

Directly I had come into the pretentious chamber of audience, and the flunky had closed the folding-doors behind me, this fascinating little prophetess began to talk, her words rippling over one another like the waves of a river; her natural excitement betraying itself in the obvious restraint of her gestures.

"I'm so glad it's you!" she exclaimed, clasping her hands together, as though in ecstasy. "Those old women bother me to death, and there have been twelve of them here this morning. Colonel Oldfield told me all about you yesterday, and I was interested at once. We must have a good long talk. Oh, do listen to that dreadful creature; she talks in scales beginning at the lower C and going up to no possible note in the music of heaven or earth. I suppose she won't go away."

Her remark, and the clapping of her little hands to equally little ears, followed upon the sound of altercation between one of the ladies in the waiting-room and the flunky of formidable mien. Apparently the lady would not depart without a *séance*, and the footman was compelling her. In the end she went, declaring the whole thing a cheat, and "that chit of a girl" a particular imposture. When the sound of her voice had died away upon the stairs, My Lady took up the thread of her remarks.

"Now," said she, "I want to have a good look at you, and you must have a good look at me. People like ourselves should know each other to begin with. Don't think I'm going to bore you with the nonsense I trade in—you are far too clever for that, and would find me out in a minute. You see, I'm like a man with a good cellar: I keep the old wine for the old birds who are not caught with chaff. That's a delightfully mixed metaphor, isn't it? and not very polite, when I think of it. But come and sit down near the light, where I can see you."

She spoke so quickly that I did not pretend to hear half of that which she said, or to answer her; but I seated myself upon the ottoman near the entrance to the conservatory; and when she had thrown open the glass doors, she herself took the low arm-chair facing me. I saw then that she wore a strange dress in the Egyptian fashion, and that her breast was all covered with jingling gold medals, while her hair was similarly ornamented.

"Come," she said, resting her head upon her hand, "I want to know from you *why* you are here. It is not for me to tell you about your life, is it?"

"I will be frank," I replied; "it is not. My life has already spoken a good deal for itself. What I did come here to see was the making of diamonds. They tell me you possess the philosopher's stone, or something near to it."

She looked at me with a penetrating gaze, and then laughed a little hardly.

"And you believed it?" she asked presently.

"Not for a moment," said I; "but I thought it was not unlikely that you had some amusing trick which you would not mind showing me. I am very much interested in jewels, you know."

"So am I," she exclaimed, but with the air of one whose mind is away from the words—"there is nothing more beautiful or more mysterious on earth than a diamond. It just seems to be a prison for lovely things of which it gives us the lights when we treat it well. And you thought I might amuse you with a trick? That was a poor compliment, wasn't it?"

The thing was said with a swift reversion of her mind to the subject, as I could see; and there was a world of humour in her eyes when she turned them on me.

"It was no poor compliment," said I, "since you have convinced such a man as Colonel Oldfield that you can make rubies. He is a judge of jewels, too."

"And a very good one," she replied; "but really there was nothing in my experiment. What I do has been done by French chemists for twenty years past. The Colonel came here with an open mind—but you, you closed the doors of yours as you came upstairs."

I protested feebly, but she did not listen to my answer.

"Yes," she exclaimed, speaking very rapidly, "I have been thinking about you as you sat there, and I am sure that I know you now. You are a man so well accustomed to steer in the shallows of your business that you never look beyond them. You make a gospel of distrust, and you consider confidence the sign of a weak intellect. You have been often deceived, for your breadth of view is not large; and you will be often deceived again. It is impossible for you to conceive beauty which is not saleable; and for romance you have no place in your heart. You have come here, saying all the way, 'I am going to interview an impostor; she will not amuse me—most possibly she will bore me. It is ten thousand to one that her experiments are all rubbish, but I will take the ten thousandth chance, in the hope that she might have found out something which I can sell—sell—sell.' Yet you are honest in a measure, since you ask me for a trick, knowing well that a trick is all you can reasonably expect from me. You are, in short, not very far removed from that dreadful person 'the pure man of business'; and you feel woefully strange already in the presence of one whose occupation is romance, and whose profession is undisguisedly practised in the offices of mystery. Do I speak the truth?"

She bent forward so that I could look straight into her eyes as she finished the excited sketch of character; and while with any other speaker my vanity had been sore wounded, I listened to her with no other feelings than those of growing admiration. The potency of her personality was beyond description; I have never met a woman who could communicate her own magnetism so quickly when she chose to talk seriously. And beyond this, I had already corrected my assumption that she was not clever. She had, indeed, one of the quickest brains I have ever dealt with.

"You are very hard on me," said I, as she waited for me to speak, "but I cannot say that you do not get to the bottom of the affair. You do me an injustice, however, when you say that my visit is purely commercial. No one in London would be more unselfishly interested than myself if any progress were made with the thousand attempts to manufacture jewels. If you have succeeded even in a small degree, your fortune is made."

"Do you think that?" she cried. "Well, a word from Mr. Bernard Sutton is a word indeed; but we shall see. Meanwhile, we are going to have some fruit and wine. Don't you find it fearfully close in here?—that's the

" OCCUPYING HERSELF IN MIXING ME AN EFFERVESCING DRAUGHT IN A
GREAT CRYSTAL GOBLET."

heat from my furnace in the conservatory there. I've had a little one put up especially for my experiments. As you were coming, we had to get the metal melted; and we've had a fire there since last night."

"You will experiment for me, then?" said I, with considerable interest.

"If you are very good," she replied, "I may show you something; but first you must taste my sherbet, and tell me all about the diamonds which I have bought and not made. You've heard, perhaps, that I waste all my money on jewellery."

I told her that I had not, but the flunky appearing at that moment, she did not pursue the subject, occupying herself in mixing me an effervescing draught in a great crystal goblet. The drink was gratifying on the hot day; and when I had taken it there was a warm coursing of blood through my veins as though I had drunk of rich Burgundy.

"Now," said she, when the man had gone, but had left the little table piled up with fruit—"now we can talk seriously. Let us carry the liquid with us—that's what Jack Lucas always calls it; he gets me that sherbet from some place in the East with an unpronounceable name. I am going to put you into an armchair, and you are not to ask a single question until I have finished. Have you got any cigarettes with you?—you may smoke if you are very good."

We went into the conservatory, which was ridiculously small, and close almost to suffocation, and there I saw many evidences of her attempt to fathom the unfathomable mysteries. There were racks with bottles round three sides of the apartment, and in the corner of the other side there stood a common little furnace such as smiths use. These, with a number of brass plates covered with hieroglyphics, some presses in steel, a basket containing strips of metal and a quantity of crystals, were her whole equipment for the business before her; but there was a low armchair in the shape of those used for dental horrors; and there she asked me to sit while she herself prepared for the undertaking.

"The first thing for you to do," said she, "is to make yourself comfortable. A man who is ill at ease is in the worst possible mental state, for he cannot concentrate himself. Just at present I want you to concentrate yourself on that cigarette and the fizzing stuff. When everything is ready I shall call out."

With this said, she set the fruit and the cup at the side of my chair, and then rolled up the sleeves of her dress quickly, putting on an apron which covered her finery; and she looked for all the world like an unusually pretty housemaid. I watched her with even a larger interest than I had done; and I remember thinking, as I settled in the great lounge, that whatever her mental claims might be upon the admiration of the city, her personal qualities were undeniable.

These were especially to be observed when she began to busy herself with the furnace and the tiny crucibles upon it, the glow of soft light seeming to emphasize the youthfulness of her perfect face, and to converge upon it as light focussed upon a picture. She had now fallen into a very serious mood, and after she had used the bellows vigorously at her fire, and placed the smallest of the crucibles upon it again, she sat herself upon a stool at the side of my chair, and resting her head upon her open hand—her favourite attitude—she spoke with evident earnestness.

"The mysteries of jewels," she exclaimed, "and the mysteries of gold have eaten the heart out of many a clever man, from Gebir to Sir Isaac Newton. If you will read the history of the philosophers, even of some in the story of that which we call the modern ages, you will find amongst the greatest the names of those who sought for an 'alkahest' or universal solvent. Even the wisest of men have hoped for a full knowledge of the arcana of metals. · Paracelsus himself believed in the fifth, or the quintessence of creation. Roger Bacon, to whom death came out of neglect, prescribed as the elixir of life gold dissolved in nitro-hydrochloric acid. Why should I tell you how science now laughs at these old philosophers, and lumps them together as little better than maniacs? Yet does she laugh at them with good reason? Is it not just possible that she will be ultimately the means of turning the laugh upon herself? In our day she has come very near to knowing of the transmutability of metals. Allotropy has turned the eyes of many back to the remoter past. The chemist is beginning to ask himself, Were these men such fools? The near future may cast a light upon long centuries of darkness. But those only will reap who come to the work with open minds, with the certain conviction that in all pertaining to this vast science we are still children. Do you follow me in this?"

"Perfectly," I replied; and assuredly a prettier lecture was never given. The girl's eyes seemed to flash lights as she warmed to her subject; her enthusiasm was so contagious that I found myself softening before it. She was earnest, at any rate; and most of her kind were quacks.

"If you grant this long premiss, and do not consider that all inquiry is necessarily useless," she continued, "you solve the greater difficulties which surround my conceptions. It remains to ask, What steps must the

chemist follow who would seek to turn from his crucible
the perfect jewel? Let us take the sapphire as an instance. It is my favourite stone, one compelling, as the
ancients declare, the wearer to all good works. Well,
the sapphire in all its beautiful tints is only a variety of
corundum, coloured by metallic oxide. It is a common
crystal, a six-sided prism terminated in a six-sided pyra-
mid. It is taken from gneiss, and we know to-day that
alumina is the basis of it, as it is the basis of so many
precious stones. Granted this, what is the work before
the chemist? Is it not simply to cast in his crucible the
crystals of the base, to colour them with the metallic
oxide, if he can, and to harden them so that they will
bear the tests? The process is a long one—it needs days
to bring it to perfection: the annealing, the polishing,
the setting—these are not work for an hour. What I
have to show you now are but the stages of it. These
you shall see and judge for yourself; but I ask you very
sincerely to weigh up this great question for yourself,
not to be led by the incredulity of the fanatic, and to believe with me that we are on the brink of a discovery
which shall pour jewels on the world as the sea casts
pebbles upon a beach."

I said nothing in answer to this remarkable delivery,
for the truth was that I watched the girl rather than
heard her words. Her earnestness, nay, her enthusiasm
was so pretty to see that all my interest seemed absorbed
in her; and now, when she rose swiftly and drew the
curtains over the windows, leaving the place illuminated
only by one rose-coloured lamp, I followed all her actions
as one follows the change of a picture.

"Let us keep away the daylight," said she, "and then
we can see the crystals forming. By-and-by I will show
you the perfect jewel. Now look."

What she did in the next few minutes I am quite unable to say, so swift were her movements and so hurried her talk. But I remember that she opened the furnace door, allowing soft rays of deep yellow light to flood the room; and then quickly she cast a dozen crystals upon the table from the glowing crucible; and from a press near to her hand she took three more and laid them on the plate. The largest of the crystals, which was blue as a sapphire, and possessed little light at a distance, she presently picked up with tiny tongs, and coming over to me, she knelt at my side, holding the jewel before my eyes, and clasping my left hand in hers. And then she cried with the wildest excitement in her voice, and her breast heaving with her emotion,—

" Oh, look at it! is there anything more beautiful on earth than a perfect sapphire ? and I made it, it is all my work, all my own ! "

While she cried thus she held my hand firmly, and the pressure of her own was hot as fire, but this I only remembered afterwards, for gradually, as I looked at the jewel critically, it took the colour and the shape of a perfect gem. It was not a large stone, perhaps one of three carats, but the longer I looked upon it the more brilliant and beautiful did it appear to be. Never had I seen more perfect shape or promise of light when set; and with the realization of the discovery my head reeled as the possibility that this mere girl had succeeded where so many had failed loomed at last before me. It was true, then, as Oldfield said, that she could manufacture a perfect jewel before his eyes. Here was one which, if well cut, I could sell for a hundred pounds. She had made that, as I could swear: why should she not make a hundred, a thousand ? My heart leaped at the conclusion.

"Tell me," said I, "you had no help in this work?"

"You saw that I had none," she cried. "Look at the other crystals; there are five of them. You have seen them come straight from the crucible—and you know

"PRESENTLY HE GAVE ONE GREAT SHOUT OF HILARITY."

that I have succeeded. Will you buy my sapphire? Buy it in proof that I have conquered you. When you return to-morrow I will tell you everything. I am exhausted now. The work always excites me terribly. My nerves are all unstrung; I can do no more to-day."

"If you will sell me the stone you hold in those tongs, I will give you fifty pounds for it," I said, concluding that, even had I been tricked, a real jewel, and a very good one, was before my eyes. But at this promise she cried out with joy, and, putting the stone in a little box with lightning speed, she handed it to me.

"Pay me to-morrow, any time," she said. "It was good of you to come here, and to listen to me. I am very grateful. When you come again you shall know all my secret. Only think well of me and be my friend."

With this she led the way quickly into her own room, and the lackey appeared in answer to her ring. The interview was at an end, abruptly as it seemed to me, and I left her with a strange feeling of dizziness, and my head burning with excitement—but her sapphire was in my pocket.

*   *   *   *   *

When I met Bracebridge, who was waiting in my rooms for me, he had an ugly leer upon his face.

"Well," said he, "I fancy my hundred's all right?"

"What hundred?" I asked.

"With Oldfield," said he. "I bet him a hundred she'd sell you a piece of glass for a sapphire; and I don't suppose you'll deny that she did it?"

"I'm not going to deny anything of the sort," said I; "she did sell me glass, and of the commonest kind. I am now seeking an undiscovered superlative. The biggest fool in London is no designation for me."

"Ah," said he, "you should take it quietly. She's done a complete dozen of us at the game. That paraphernalia which Jack Lucas rigged up in her conservatory for her is the medium, I fancy. Lucas, you know, is a professor or something at Emmanuel, Cambridge. He taught her all that jargon about crystals."

"But," said I, as I pitched her glass into the fireplace, "what I want to know is, how did I come to think that the stuff was real? I could have sworn to it."

"So could we all," he replied, with a great burst of laughter; "but I'll tell you in a word—she hypnotised you. I always said you were a grand subject."

I looked him in the face for a minute, during which he made an heroic attempt to be serious. But it was too much for him. Presently he gave one great shout of hilarity which you could have heard halfway down the street, and then rolled about in his chair uncontrollably.

"You seem to find it amusing," said I, "but I fail to catch the point."

"You'll be seeing it by-and-by," said he, and at that he went off to the club to be first with it.

THE END.

Breinigsville, PA USA
21 September 2009
224442BV00003B/129/P